Praise for

Milton Friedman on Freedom

"Milton Friedman lives on because his ideas are forever and his expository skills are unsurpassed, as shown in this book of special importance in today's world."

—**George P. Shultz,** Thomas W. and Susan B. Ford Distinguished Fellow, Hoover Institution, Stanford University, former US Secretary of State, Labor, and Treasury, and director, Office of Management and Budget

"We live in an age when political, economic, religious and speech freedoms are both under attack and taken for granted. That makes these penetrating insights and trenchant analyses by their great champion, Milton Friedman, essential reading for all, both those who value freedom's great blessings and those who don't but should."

—**Michael J. Boskin,** Tully M. Friedman Professor of Economics at Stanford University and former chairman of the President's Council of Economic Advisers

"At a moment when free societies and their defenders are under growing ideological assault, Milton Friedman's incisive essays powerfully remind us of what it means to be free—and why it matters. This is a luminous, timely, and necessary book."

—**George H. Nash,** historian, author of *The Conservative Intellectual Movement in America Since 1945* and a three-volume biography of Herbert Hoover, and a senior fellow at the Russell Kirk Center for Cultural Renewal

Milton Friedman on Freedom

Milton Friedman on Freedom

Selections from
The Collected Works of Milton Friedman

Compiled and Edited by
Robert Leeson and Charles G. Palm

Foreword by
John B. Taylor

HOOVER INSTITUTION PRESS
STANFORD UNIVERSITY   STANFORD, CALIFORNIA

With its eminent scholars and world-renowned library and archives, the Hoover Institution seeks to improve the human condition by advancing ideas that promote economic opportunity and prosperity while securing and safeguarding peace for America and all mankind. The views expressed in its publications are entirely those of the authors and do not necessarily reflect the views of the staff, officers, or Board of Overseers of the Hoover Institution.

hoover.org

Hoover Institution Press Publication No. 677
Hoover Institution at Leland Stanford Junior University, Stanford, California, 94305-6003

For original publication information and credits for individual essays reprinted herein, please refer to the Bibliographical Notes section on pages 227–230.

First printing 2017
First paperback edition 2023
29 28 27 26 25 24 23   10 9 8 7 6 5 4

Manufactured in the United States of America

Cataloging-in-Publication Data is available from the Library of Congress.
ISBN 978-0-8179-2034-0 (cloth)
ISBN 978-0-8179-2035-7 (paper)
ISBN 978-0-8179-2036-4 (epub)
ISBN 978-0-8179-2037-1 (mobi)
ISBN 978-0-8179-2038-8 (PDF)

CONTENTS

Contents

PREFACE

When Milton Friedman died on November 16, 2006, at age ninety-four, Margaret Thatcher said of him, "Milton Friedman revived the economics of liberty when it had all but been forgotten. He was an intellectual freedom fighter."

In these fifteen essays, authored during the course of nearly forty years, we have attempted to present Milton Friedman's views on freedom in a comprehensive and coherent way. Freedom imbued virtually all his writings. In most of them, however, he discussed it indirectly as it applied to specific policy questions. Only in occasional works, as he did in these fifteen pieces, did he write on freedom with a primary or theoretical focus, and never did he express in a single essay all his views on the subject. By bringing together the fifteen works in this volume, we have tried to capture all his views on freedom and, in doing so, to present a complete picture of his thinking about the value that formed the moral foundation of his intellectual life.

The writings in this volume have been selected from *The Collected Works of Milton Friedman,* which we have compiled and edited for publication by the Hoover Institution on its website. *The Collected Works* include all of Friedman's published scientific and public policy writings as well as significant unpublished manuscripts—nearly 1,500 pieces totaling more than five million words. In addition to *The Collected Works,* the Hoover Institution site includes a substantial selection of Friedman's personal papers residing in the Hoover Institution Archives: correspondence, unpublished manuscripts, photographs, audio and television recordings, and other materials. By bringing these materials together in an organized way, the Hoover Institution has provided interested citizens, students, advanced scholars, and public policy makers access to more than seventy years of Friedman's works and ideas that will continue to be relevant far into the future.

We wish to acknowledge the Earhart Foundation, Roger Mertz, and Henrietta Fankhauser, who generously contributed financial support to our work and who share our interest in Milton Friedman. We also wish to thank Hoover Institution administrators and staff who assisted us in this effort, including Thomas Gilligan and John Raisian, the current and previous directors of the Hoover Institution, as well as Eric Wakin, Christopher Dauer, Gloria Valentine, Linda Bernard, Lisa Miller, Elizabeth Phillips, Carol Leadenham, Paige Minister, and Russell Rader.

Robert Leeson
Charles G. Palm

FOREWORD

In this book Robert Leeson and Charles Palm have assembled an amazing collection of Milton Friedman's best works on freedom. Even more amazing is that the selection represents only 1 percent of the 1,500 works by Friedman that Leeson and Palm have put online in a user-friendly format—and an even smaller percentage if you include their archive of Friedman's audio and television recordings, correspondence, and other writings.

This book and the larger online collection are sorely needed and very welcome. Milton Friedman deserves to be read in the original by generation after generation. I have found that people now tend to channel Friedman to support their own views, which sometimes are contrary to his actual views. With so much now readily available, everyone will find it easier to remember and learn from what he actually wrote and said. I think readers will find the book refreshing whether or not they are already familiar with Friedman's work.

It is a special pleasure to have the beautiful freedom essays packed into one lean volume. Leeson and Palm have usefully arranged the essays chronologically, enabling the reader to trace real-world developments over time and to see how Friedman reacted to these developments and indeed influenced them. In each essay Friedman focuses on a particular aspect or idea of freedom; throughout the volume he illustrates the abstract ideas with real-world examples and stories, from Alexander Hamilton's call for trade protection in 1791 to Friedman's own experiences in bringing an end to the military draft or promoting school vouchers nearly two centuries later.

Appropriately, the book starts with one of Friedman's first articles focused on freedom. Writing in the 1950s Friedman reminds us that liberalism in the original classical sense fundamentally "takes freedom of the individual—really, of the family—as its ultimate value" and recalls "Schumpeter['s] remarks [that], 'as a supreme if unintended compliment, the enemies of the system of private enterprise have thought it wise to appropriate its label.'"

The essays then go on to develop the connection between economic freedom and other freedoms. Friedman firmly believed that "economic freedom, in and of itself, is an extremely important part of total freedom." Indeed, the loss of total freedom caused by restrictions on economic freedom were at least as much of a concern to Freidman as the loss of economic efficiency caused by such restrictions. He writes that "a citizen of the United States who under the laws of various states is not free to follow the occupation of his own choosing unless he can get a license for it, is likewise being deprived of an essential part of his freedom."

I like the examples that show how reductions in economic freedom through government subsidies or regulations stifle freedom of speech. He writes that "the only people who are really effectively free at the moment are a subset of long-tenured professors in leading universities. Only a subset. . . . Let us suppose that you are a professor of medicine and your research is being financed by the National Institute of Health or the National Science Foundation and you personally believe that it's wrong for government to subsidize medical research. Would you really feel free to get up and make that statement in public?" And he gives the example of Gerald Ford's Whip Inflation Now program. Taken as a whole the program was "pretty silly," Friedman argues, yet not one business leader spoke out against it. The reason, he argued, was concern about such things as the "IRS getting ready to come and audit" or "the Department of Justice standing only too ready to launch an antitrust suit."

Friedman also reminds us that periods of freedom are rare in the long span of history and that free market systems and political freedom tend to be unstable: "The direction has been away from freedom and not towards it. There isn't any doubt about the fact." He gives examples from Chile and the United Kingdom; in his essays from the 1970s he sounds many warnings for the United States as in the piece "The Fragility of Freedom."

His comments on the role of government in a free society and on how his approach differs from other champions of free markets are particularly interesting. He argues that there is a "utopian strand in libertarianism. You cannot simply describe the utopian solution and leave it to somebody else how we get from here to there. That's not only a practical problem. It's a problem of the responsibilities that we have."

He argues for an empirical approach in which one is tolerant of views one disagrees with and tests them with data. He writes that "there is no doubt in my mind that Ludwig von Mises has done more to spread the fundamental ideas of free markets than any other individual. There is no doubt in my mind that nobody has done more than Ayn Rand to develop a popular following for many of these ideas. And yet there is also no doubt that both of them were extremely intolerant." He suggests instead that objective empirical work will help resolve differences and disagreements.

The chronological order of the book brings attention to an important question about the connection between the world of ideas and the world of practical policy. Indeed, the final essay in the book, written jointly by Friedman and his wife, Rose, brings many of his ideas together and raises important questions about our current predicaments and future directions. The Friedmans put forth the hypothesis that there is a close connection between the world of ideas and the world of practical policy. They note a historical pattern: Swings in the tide of ideas about freedom are followed, with a long lag, by swings in the tide of applications of the idea. But just as the applications of the ideas are reaching a peak, there is a countermovement against freedom, which in turn affects the real world with an equally long lag.

They first describe the rise of laissez-faire from 1840 to 1930, which followed the Adam Smith tide that began in 1776. They then describe the rise of the welfare state from 1930 to 1980, which followed the Fabian tide that began in 1885, then the resurgence of free markets beginning in 1980 following the Hayek Tide. (These are their dates for the United States; they differ slightly from their dates for Britain.) Writing in 1988, they noted that each tide lasted between fifty and one hundred years.

But with developments since 1988, readers of this book must wonder whether the most recent tide was cut short at twenty or thirty years, much less fifty or a hundred. I have written that there has been a change in both the ideas and the policy tides in recent years in the United States and in Britain. Policy has moved away from the principles of economic freedom, a move closely associated with similar shift in the world of ideas.

There is little doubt that the events surrounding the global financial crisis were a factor in the recent shifts. The Friedmans argue in the final essay of the book that the panic of 1837 in which "many, perhaps most, government enterprises went bankrupt . . . discrediting government enterprise" was a catalytic factor in the laissez-faire tide. They also argue that the Great Depression of the 1930s, by discrediting private enterprise, was a catalytic factor in the rise of the welfare state. Perhaps the global financial crisis has played a similar role, or perhaps the tide is turning again. Either way, the lessons learned from the essays on freedom in this book tell us that it is not a time for complacency. Indeed, Friedman's broad historical sweep tells us it is never a time for complacency.

John B. Taylor
George P. Shultz Senior Fellow in Economics,
Hoover Institution, and Mary and Robert Raymond
Professor of Economics at Stanford University

ONE

LIBERALISM, OLD STYLE

(1955)

Liberalism, as it developed in the seventeenth and eighteenth centuries and flowered in the nineteenth, puts major emphasis on the freedom of individuals to control their own destinies. Individualism is its creed; collectivism and tyranny its enemy. The state exists to protect individuals from coercion by other individuals or groups and to widen the range within which individuals can exercise their freedom; it is purely instrumental and has no significance in and of itself. Society is a collection of individuals, and the whole is no greater than the sum of its parts. The ultimate values are the values of the individuals who form the society; there are no super-individual values or ends. Nations may be convenient administrative units; nationalism is an alien creed.

In politics, liberalism expressed itself as a reaction against authoritarian regimes. Liberals favored limiting the rights of hereditary rulers, establishing democratic parliamentary institutions, extending the franchise, and guaranteeing civil rights. They favored such measures both for their own sake, as a direct expression of essential political freedoms, and as a means of facilitating the adoption of liberal economic measures.

In economic policy, liberalism expressed itself as a reaction against government intervention in economic affairs. Liberals favored free competition at home and free trade among nations.

They regarded the organization of economic activity through free private enterprise operating in a competitive market as a direct expression of essential economic freedoms and as important also in facilitating the preservation of political liberty. They regarded free trade among nations as a means of eliminating conflicts that might otherwise produce war. Just as within a country, individuals following their own interests under the pressures of competition indirectly promote the interests of the whole; so, between countries, individuals following their own interests under conditions of free trade indirectly promote the interests of the world as a whole. By providing free access to goods, services, and resources on the same terms to all, free trade would knit the world into a single economic community.

"Liberalism" has taken on a very different meaning in the twentieth century and particularly in the United States. This difference is least in the concrete political forms favored: both the nineteenth-century liberal and the twentieth-century liberal favor or profess to favor parliamentary forms, nearly universal adult franchise, and the protection of civil rights. But even in politics there are some not unimportant differences: in any issue involving a choice between centralization or decentralization of political responsibility, the nineteenth-century liberal will resolve any doubt in favor of strengthening the importance of local governments at the expense of the central government; for, to him, the main desideratum is to strengthen the defenses against arbitrary government and to protect individual freedom as much as possible; the twentieth-century liberal will resolve the same doubt in favor of increasing the power of the central government at the expense of local government; for, to him, the main desideratum is to strengthen the power of the government to do "good for" the people.

The difference is much sharper in economic policy where liberalism now stands for almost the opposite of its earlier meaning. Nineteenth-century liberalism favors private enterprise and a minimum of government intervention. Twentieth-century liberalism distrusts the market in all its manifestations and favors widespread government intervention in, and control over, economic activity. Nineteenth-century liberalism favors individualist means to foster its individualist objectives. Twentieth-century liberalism favors collectivist means while professing individualist objectives. And its objectives are individualist in a different sense; its keynote is welfare, not freedom. As Schumpeter remarks, "as a supreme, if unintended, compliment, the enemies of the system of private enterprise have thought it wise to appropriate its label."[1] The rest of this article is devoted entirely to liberalism in its original meaning, and the term will be used throughout in that sense.

Political liberalism and economic liberalism derive from a single philosophy. Yet they have frequently led independent lives in application, which suggests that their relation to one another deserves examination in the realm of ideas as well. During the nineteenth century, many countries adopted large elements of economic liberalism, yet maintained political forms that were neither liberal nor developing at any rapid pace in a liberal direction. Russia and Japan are perhaps the outstanding examples. During the twentieth century, countries that have achieved and maintained most of the concrete elements of the liberal political program have been moving away from liberal and toward collectivist economic policies. Great Britain is the most striking example; certainly for the first half of this century, the general drift of British economic policies has been toward greater direct intervention and control by the state; this drift has been checked in the past few years, but whether the check is more than transitory remains to be seen. Norway, Sweden, and, with a lag of several decades, the United States, exhibit much the same tendencies.

As already noted, liberal thinkers and writers in the nineteenth century regarded political reforms as in large part a means of achieving economic liberalism. The earlier political forms concentrated political power in the hands of groups whose special interests were opposed to such measures of economic liberalism as free trade. Let all the people have a vote, and there would be, so liberals like James Mill argued, no special interest. And since the general interest was simply the interest of all the individuals composing the society, and these in turn would be furthered most effectively by economic liberalism, democracy could be expected to rid itself of the dead hand of government and to give maximum scope to the invisible hand of self-interest.

In the twentieth century, a group of liberal thinkers, especially Henry Simons, Ludwig von Mises, and Friedrich von Hayek, has emphasized that this relation also runs in reverse: that economic liberalism is a means of achieving political freedom. Economic liberalism alone does not guarantee political freedom—witness the examples of Russia and Japan cited earlier. But economic liberalism is, it is argued, an indispensable prerequisite for political freedom. Historically, there are no countries that enjoyed any substantial measure of political freedom that did not also practice a substantial measure of economic liberalism. Analytically, the preservation of political freedom requires protection against the concentration of power; it requires the existence of largely independent loci of power. Political power by its nature tends to be concentrated; economic power can be highly deconcentrated if it is organized by means of an impersonal market; economic power can thus be an independent offset to political power. Let both economic and political power be in the same hands and the only protection of political freedom is the goodwill of those in power—a frail recourse, particularly in view of the corrupting influence of power and the talents that make for political survival.

A few examples may clarify the asserted relation between economic and political freedom, though they cannot of course demonstrate it. A characteristic of a politically free society is that proponents of radical reform in the structure of the society are permitted to express their views and to seek to persuade their fellows. It is a testimonial to the freedom of the United States that socialist and communist magazines and papers are published. Suppose a change to a collectivist economic society with government control of the bulk of economic activity. How could the proponents of a return to capitalism secure the resources with which to publish a magazine urging their point of view? Through a government fund for dissidents? Through the collection of small sums from millions of government employees? If they had the resources in the form of funds, what guarantee could they have that the government would sell them paper on the same terms as it does to others? In an economically liberal society, it is possible to get the general resources with which to spread dissenting views either by subsidies from a small number of individuals or by selling a magazine or other publication to many; if there is a reasonable chance that enough people will want to buy a magazine expressing the minority view to make it profitable, even people who disagree fundamentally with the view will in their own self-interest provide the resources to make its establishment possible. In effect, there are thousands or millions of independent loci of power to decide whether an idea is worth trying to promote, rather than the few or one in a political structure. And given the general resources, there is no further obstacle: in a thoroughly free market, the sellers of paper do not know whether the paper is going to the *Daily Worker* or the *Foundation for Economic Education*. Perhaps some similar impersonal and effective guarantees of freedom to promote dissenting views could be contrived for a collectivist society; certainly no proponents of such a society have yet suggested any or even faced this problem squarely.

As another example, consider those individuals who have lost or resigned government jobs in the United States in recent years because they were or were accused of being Communists. Government employment in our society is not a right, and it is entirely appropriate that at least certain governmental positions should not be open to actual or suspected Communists. It is easy also to see how strong public feeling can lead to a closing of all government posts to Communists. Yet the maintenance of political freedom surely requires that people be free not only to believe in but also to advocate communism; those of us who abhor communism do so in part precisely because we know it would not grant us freedom to express contrary views; our defense against communism is to persuade our fellow citizens of its evil, not to suppress its advocates. But if government employment were the only employment, nominal freedom to express extreme views would be a mockery. The exercise of this freedom would be at a prohibitive price—namely, giving up the possibility of earning a living. By contrast, in the existing society those who have left government employment have had a wide variety of other opportunities. The way a private market economy protects these opportunities is revealed most clearly by considering an individual who goes into farming and produces, say, wheat. The purchasers of the wheat do not know whether it has been produced by a Communist or a Fascist, a white man or a Negro; they could hardly discriminate if they wanted to. The competitive market in this way separates economic activity from intellectual or political activity; the more competitive the market, the more sharply it does so. It is a paradox that minorities who have in this way the most to gain from a competitive society have contributed unduly large numbers to the ranks of its opponents.

Many writers who emphasize the importance of economic liberalism as a prerequisite for political freedom have interpreted tendencies toward collectivism in recent decades as betokening a trend toward political "serfdom." They may yet be proved right. So far, however, the relation they stress has manifested itself mostly in a very different way: namely, the collectivist tendencies have been checked because they tended to interfere with civil and political freedom; when the conflict has been reasonably clear, the collectivist policy has frequently given way. Perhaps the most striking example is the British experience with the compulsory allocation of labor. Socialist economic thinking in the postwar period called for compulsory allocation of labor to achieve "social priorities"; though some compulsory powers were provided by law, they were never widely used; the powers themselves were permitted to lapse; and the whole character of attempted economic policy changed because compulsory allocation of labor so clearly interfered with widely and deeply cherished civil rights.

We turn now to a more detailed examination of the content of liberalism, particularly economic liberalism, and of the role it assigns to the state. This examination deals primarily with the principles that liberalism provides for judging social action. Any set of concrete proposals that these principles lead liberals to favor will vary with the particular circumstances of time and place and, consequently, are less fundamental and invariant than the principles themselves. There is some possibility of being reasonably comprehensive with respect to principles; none, with respect to concrete proposals.

Principles for social action must be based on both ultimate values and on a conception of the nature of man and the world. Liberalism takes freedom of the individual—really, of the family—as its ultimate value. It conceives of man as a responsible individual who is egocentric, in the sense not of being selfish or self-centered but rather of placing greater reliance on his own values than on those of his neighbors. It takes as the major problem of modern society the achievement of liberty and individual responsibility in a world that requires the co-ordination of many of millions of people in production to make full use of modern knowledge and technology. The challenge is to reconcile individual freedom with widespread interdependence.

The liberal answer derives from the elementary—yet even today little understood—proposition that both sides to an economic transaction can benefit from it; that a gain to a purchaser need not be at the expense of a loss to the seller. If the transaction is voluntary and informed, both sides benefit; the buyer gets something he values more than whatever he gives up, and so does the seller. In consequence, voluntary exchange is a way to get cooperation among individuals without coercion. The reliance on voluntary exchange, which means on a free market mechanism, is thus central to the liberal creed.

The working model which embodies this vision of a society organized through voluntary exchange is a free private enterprise exchange economy. The elementary social unit—the family or household—is generally too small for efficient use of modern productive techniques. Accordingly, the productive unit takes the form of an enterprise which purchases productive services—labor, the use of capital, and so on—from households and other enterprises and sells the goods or services it produces to households and other enterprises. The introduction of such enterprises does not change the strictly voluntary and individual character of the cooperation, provided two conditions are satisfied: first, the enterprises are *private,* which means that the ultimate locus of authority and responsibility is an individual or a group of individuals; second, individuals are *free* to sell or not sell their services or to buy or not buy products from particular enterprises, which means, also, that they are *free* to establish new enterprises.

The final point deserves special emphasis in view of the widespread misunderstanding of it. "Free" in the liberal conception of free enterprise means freedom to establish enterprises to do whatever they want. This is one of those familiar cases in which absolute freedom is impossible because the freedom of some limits the freedom of others: the freedom of existing enterprises to do whatever they want, including combining to keep new entrants out or to fix prices and divide markets, may limit the freedom of others to establish new enterprises or to make the best bargain they can. When such a conflict arises, the liberal tradition regards freedom of entry and of competition as basic; it therefore justifies state action to preserve competition and to make selling a product of higher quality or at a lower price the only means whereby existing enterprises can prevent new enterprises from being established. The most difficult practical problem in this area and one on which liberals have spoken with many tongues is combinations among laborers—the trade union problem.

In the free enterprise exchange economy envisaged by liberalism, the primary role of government is to preserve the rules of the game by enforcing contracts, preventing coercion, providing a stable monetary framework, and, as just noted, keeping markets free. Beyond this there are only three major grounds on which government intervention is justified: (1) "natural monopoly" or similar market imperfections; (2) the existence of substantial "neighborhood effects"; (3) protection of children and other irresponsible individuals.

An exchange is "voluntary" only when essentially equivalent alternatives exist: when an individual can choose whether to buy from one enterprise or another, to work for one enterprise or another. Monopoly means the absence of alternatives and thus is incompatible with strictly voluntary exchange. Monopoly may arise from combinations among enterprises in circumstances where competition is entirely feasible, and, as already noted, liberal tradition justifies state intervention to preserve competition in such cases. But monopoly may also be "natural," as in the textbook examples of a single spring providing drinking water, or of a product subject to such large economies of scale that the most efficient productive unit is large enough to serve the whole market. The only available alternatives are then all bad: government regulation, government ownership, or private monopoly, and the problem is to choose the least of these evils. As might be expected, liberals have no clear-cut answer. Henry Simons, after observing in the United States the consequences of government regulation of such alleged natural monopolies as the railroads, concluded that government ownership was the least of the evils when monopoly was inevitable. Walter Eucken, after observing in Germany the consequences of government ownership, concluded that government control was the least of the evils. And some have argued that in a dynamic world private monopoly may well be, citing the case of the regulation of transportation in the United States as their principle example. The Interstate Commerce Commission was established to protect the public against the railroads when railroads probably did have a large element of natural monopoly. The development of highway and air transport has largely eliminated any natural monopoly element in railroads, yet instead of the abolition of the Interstate Commerce Commission, government control has been extended to these other transportation media. The ICC has become a means of protecting the railroads from the competition of trucks instead of the public from the absence of competition. Fortunately for the possibility of a liberal society, the area within which natural monopoly is a serious problem is exceedingly limited, so that no large amount of government intervention is called for on this score. In practice, the claim of natural monopoly is more often an excuse for intervention desired on other grounds than a valid justification for intervention.

A different kind of threat to strictly voluntary exchange arises from the so-called "neighborhood effect." This occurs when the action of one individual imposes significant costs on other individuals for which it is not feasible to make him compensate them or yields significant gains to other individuals for which it is not feasible to make them compensate him. A simple example is that of an individual polluting a stream. He has in effect forced other individuals further down the stream to exchange good water for bad: they clearly would have been willing to do so for a price; but it is not feasible to make this exchange the subject of voluntary agreement. Another rather different example, is education. The education of a child is regarded as benefiting not only the child and his parents but also other members of society, since some minimum level of education is a prerequisite for a stable and democratic society. Yet it is not feasible to identify the particular individuals benefited by the education of any particular child, much less the money value of the benefit, and so to charge for the services rendered. In consequence there is justification on liberal grounds for the state requiring some minimum amount of education for all children, even though this is above the amount parents would otherwise provide, and for meeting some of the cost of education from taxes imposed on all members of society.

Of course, all actions of an individual involve some "unborne costs" and "inappropriable benefits" to third parties. It is always a question of judgment whether these are sufficiently great in any particular case to justify state intervention; the state too will be plagued by the difficulties of identifying costs and benefits that prevent voluntary exchange and there are other costs of state action. The liberal philosophy thus gives no hard and fast line separating appropriate from inappropriate state action in this area. But it does emphasize that, in deciding any particular case, one general cost of state action—one general neighborhood effect, as it were—must always be taken into account; namely, that the extension of state action involves an encroachment on individual freedom. The liberal regards this as a count against any proposal for state action, though by no means a fatal obstacle to it, and hence requires a clear net balance of gains over other costs before regarding the state action as justified.

The third ground on which liberalism justifies state intervention derives from an ambiguity in the ultimate objective rather than from the difficulty of achieving fully voluntary exchange. The belief in freedom is for "responsible" individuals; children and insane people cannot be regarded as "responsible." In general, this problem is avoided for children by treating the family as the basic unit of society and so regarding the parents as responsible for their children. In considerable measure, however, this procedure rests on expediency rather than principle. The problem of drawing a reasonable line between action justified on these paternalistic grounds and action that conflicts with the freedom of responsible individuals is clearly one to which no fully satisfactory—and certainly no simple—answer can be given.

A few additional examples may clarify the bearing of these principles in judging particular acts of social policy. Consider first a group of measures that clearly conflict with liberal principles: tariffs, direct controls of imports and exports, exchange control, general price controls. None of these can be justified on any of the grounds for state intervention that we have listed. Each represents an interference with the freedom of individuals to engage in any transactions that they want to and thus involve a direct interference with essential freedoms. An extreme case that brings out this feature strikingly is the "tourist allowance" incorporated in the exchange control regulations of a number of countries; as the *Economist* puts it, "it sets a limit on the length of time that even the most economical British resident can choose to spend abroad without asking the permission of some bureaucrat." Finally most of these measures prevent the market from operating effectively and thus threaten the heart of the liberal system. For example, if a legal maximum price is established below the level that would otherwise prevail, a shortage will inevitably follow (as in housing under rent control); some method other than the free market will have to be used to ration the available amount and further government intervention replacing the market is set in train.

A second rather different example is medicine. As already noted, significant neighborhood effects justify substantial public health activities: maintaining the purity of water, assuring proper sewage disposal, controlling contagious diseases. There is little or no justification on these grounds for state intervention into private medicine: the care and treatment of individuals. Under liberal principles, this is a function the market can and should perform. To the argument of the proponent of socialized medicine that there is great uncertainty about possible medical bills, the liberal will reply that the market is perfectly capable of providing private insurance; if people don't want to pay the premium, that is their free choice. To the argument that people don't get as much medical service as is "good" for them, the liberal will reply that each man should judge for himself—not that he is necessarily the best judge but that he should make his own mistakes; insofar as we think he is making the wrong decision, there is no objection to telling him what we think and trying to persuade him, but there is no justification for making his decision.

A third example is public housing. It may be that certain types of housing (e.g., dense slum districts) impose higher costs of police and fire protection on the community. This literal "neighborhood effect," since its source can be identified, would justify higher taxes on such property than on others to meet those extra costs; it hardly justifies subsidies to housing. The main argument for public subsidy to housing is surely paternalistic: people "need" or "deserve" better housing, and it is appropriate to use public funds to provide housing. The liberal will object on two different levels. Given that some people are to be subsidized, why not give them the subsidy in general purchasing power and let them spend it as they will? Why say to them, we will give you a gift if you take it in the form of housing but not otherwise? Does this not involve an unnecessary restriction on their freedom? Second, he will question the redistribution of income itself that is involved in such a program; indeed, one advantage of making the subsidy explicit is that it would make clear what groups are being subsidized. Government relief of poverty, the liberal will support and welcome, primarily on the explicitly paternalistic ground of taking care of the irresponsible. But the more or less indiscriminate transfer of income involved in large-scale public housing schemes, he will regard as undermining individual responsibility. The way to reduce inequality, he will urge, is not by the misleading palliative of sharing the wealth but by improving the workings of the market, strengthening competition, and widening opportunities for individuals to make the most of their own qualities.

These two final examples illustrate how the central virtue of a liberal society is at the same time a major source of the objections to it: a liberal society gives people what they want instead of what a particular group thinks they ought to want or thinks is "good" for them; it makes it equally difficult for the benevolent and the malevolent to shape other people in their own image. At bottom of most arguments against the market is lack of belief in freedom—at least for other people—as an end.

Adam Smith provides an excellent summary of the preceding discussion of the role of the state in a liberal society:

> Every man, as long as he does not violate the laws of justice, is left perfectly free to pursue his own interest his own way, and to bring both his industry and capital into competition with those of any other man, or order of men. The sovereign is completely discharged from a duty, in the attempting to perform which he

must always be exposed to innumerable delusions, and for the proper performance of which no human wisdom or knowledge could ever be sufficient; the duty of superintending the industry of private people, and of directing it towards the employments most suitable to the interest of the society. According to the system of natural liberty, the sovereign has only three duties to attend to; three duties of great importance, indeed, but plain and intelligible to common understanding: first, the duty of protecting the society from the violence and invasion of other independent societies; secondly, the duty of protecting, as far as possible, every member of the society from the injustice or oppression of every other member of it, or the duty of establishing an exact administration of justice; and, thirdly, the duty of erecting and maintaining certain public works and certain public institutions, which it can never be for the interest of any individual, or small number of individuals, to erect and maintain; because the profit could never repay the expense to any individual or small number of individuals, though it may frequently do much more than repay it to a great society.[2]

Notes

Editor's Note: We included in *Collier's 1954 Year Book* an article on conservatism by Russell Kirk, who at that time had recently published his book *The Conservative Mind* (Regnery, 1953). One of our readers, on seeing Mr. Kirk's article, wrote to us suggesting the desirability of an article on liberalism. The suggestion seemed good to us: to carry it out we have arranged the following discussion.

The first article, by Milton Friedman, professor of economics, the University of Chicago, presents liberalism as it was when laissez-faire was the dominant doctrine and state controls were relatively unimportant. The second, by Seymour Harris, professor of economics, Harvard University, argues that such liberalism is outmoded both in theory and in practice and presents the case for the "new liberalism" of the period from the New Deal to the present.

1. Joseph A. Schumpeter, *History of Economic Analysis* (1954), p. 394.

2. Adam Smith, *An Inquiry into the Nature and Causes of the Wealth of Nations.* London: Methuen & Co. Ltd., 1930. II, 184–85.

TWO

THE RELATION BETWEEN ECONOMIC FREEDOM AND POLITICAL FREEDOM

(1962)

It is widely believed that politics and economics are separate and largely unconnected; that individual freedom is a political problem and material welfare an economic problem; and that any kind of political arrangements can be combined with any kind of economic arrangements. The chief contemporary manifestation of this idea is the advocacy of "democratic socialism" by many who condemn out of hand the restrictions on individual freedom imposed by "totalitarian socialism" in Russia and who are persuaded that it is possible for a country to adopt the essential features of Russian economic arrangements and yet ensure individual freedom through political arrangements. The thesis of this chapter is that such a view is a delusion, that there is an intimate connection between economics and politics, that only certain combinations of political and economic arrangements are possible, and that, in particular, a society that is socialist cannot also be democratic in the sense of guaranteeing individual freedom.

Economic arrangements play a dual role in the promotion of a free society. On the one hand, freedom in economic arrangements is itself a component of freedom broadly understood, so economic freedom is an end in itself. Secondly, economic freedom is also an indispensable means toward the achievement of political freedom.

The first of these roles of economic freedom needs special emphasis because intellectuals in particular have a strong bias against regarding this aspect of freedom as important. They tend to express contempt for what they regard as material aspects of life and to regard their own pursuit of allegedly higher values as on a different plane of significance and as deserving of special attention. For most citizens of the country, however, if not for the intellectual, the direct importance of economic freedom is at least comparable in significance to the indirect importance of economic freedom as a means to political freedom.

The citizen of Great Britain, who after World War II was not permitted to spend his vacation in the United States because of exchange control, was being deprived of an essential freedom no less than the citizen of the United States who was denied the opportunity to spend his vacation in Russia because of his political views. The one was ostensibly an economic limitation on freedom and the other a political limitation, yet there is no essential difference between the two.

The citizen of the United States who is compelled by law to devote something like 10 percent of his income to the purchase of a particular kind of retirement contract, administered by the government, is being deprived of a corresponding part of his personal freedom. How strongly this deprivation may be felt and its closeness to the deprivation of religious freedom, which all would regard as "civil" or "political" rather than "economic," were dramatized by an episode involving a group of farmers of the Amish sect. On grounds of principle, this group regarded compulsory federal old-age programs as an infringement of their personal individual freedom and refused to pay taxes or accept benefits. As a result, some of their livestock were sold by auction in to satisfy claims for Social Security levies. True, the number of citizens who regard compulsory old-age insurance as a deprivation of freedom may be few, but the believer in freedom has never counted noses.

A citizen of the United States who under the laws of various states is not free to follow the occupation of his own choosing unless he can get a license for it is likewise being deprived of an essential part of his freedom. So is the man who would like to exchange some of his goods with, say, a Swiss for a watch but is prevented from doing so by a quota. So also is the Californian who was thrown into jail for selling Alka-Seltzer at a price below that set by the manufacturer under so-called fair trade laws. So also is the farmer who cannot grow the amount of wheat he wants. And so on. Clearly, economic freedom, in and of itself, is an extremely important part of total freedom.

Viewed as a means to the end of political freedom, economic arrangements are important because of their effect on the concentration or dispersion of power. The kind of economic organization that provides economic freedom directly, namely, competitive capitalism, also promotes political freedom because it separates economic power from political power and in this way enables the one to offset the other.

Historical evidence speaks with a single voice on the relation between political freedom and a free market. I know of no example in time or place of a society that has been marked by a large measure of political freedom that has not also used something comparable to a free market to organize the bulk of economic activity.

Because we live in a largely free society, we tend to forget how limited is the span of time and the part of the globe for which there has ever been anything like political freedom: the typical state of mankind is tyranny, servitude, and misery. The nineteenth century and early twentieth century in the Western world stand out as striking exceptions to the general trend of historical development. Political freedom in this instance clearly came along with the free market and the development of capitalist institutions. So also did political freedom in the golden age of Greece and in the early days of the Roman era.

History suggests only that capitalism is a necessary condition for political freedom. Clearly it is not a sufficient condition. Fascist Italy and Fascist Spain, Germany at various times in the past seventy years, Japan before World Wars I and II, and tsarist Russia in the decades before World War I are all societies that cannot conceivably be described as politically free. Yet in each private enterprise was the dominant form of economic organization. It is therefore clearly possible to have economic arrangements that are fundamentally capitalist and political arrangements that are not free.

Even in those societies, the citizenry had a good deal more freedom than citizens of a modern totalitarian state like Russia or Nazi Germany, in which economic totalitarianism is combined with political totalitarianism. Even in Russia under the tsars, it was possible for some citizens, under some circumstances, to change their jobs without getting permission from political authority because capitalism and the existence of private property provided some check to the centralized power of the state.

The relation between political and economic freedom is complex and by no means unilateral. In the early nineteenth century, Bentham and the Philosophical Radicals were inclined to regard political freedom as a means to economic freedom. They believed that the masses were being hampered by the restrictions that were being imposed on them and that if political reform gave the bulk of the people the vote, they would do what was good for them, which was to vote for laissez-faire. In retrospect one cannot say that they were wrong. There was a large measure of political reform that was accompanied by economic reform in the direction of a great deal of laissez-faire. An enormous increase in the well-being of the masses followed this change in economic arrangements.

The triumph of Benthamite liberalism in nineteenth-century England was followed by a reaction toward increasing intervention by government in economic affairs. This tendency to collectivism was greatly accelerated, both in England and elsewhere, by the two world wars. Welfare rather than freedom became the dominant note in democratic countries. Recognizing the implicit threat to individualism, the intellectual descendants of the Philosophical Radicals—Dicey, Mises, Hayek, and Simons, to mention only a few—feared that a continued movement toward centralized control of economic activity would prove *The Road to Serfdom,* as Hayek entitled his penetrating analysis of the process. Their emphasis was on economic freedom as a means toward political freedom.

Events since the end of World War II display still a different relation between economic and political freedom. Collectivist economic planning has indeed interfered with individual freedom. At least in some countries, however, the result has not been the suppression of freedom but the reversal of economic policy. England again provides the most striking example. The turning point was perhaps the "control of engagements" order which, despite great misgivings, the Labour Party found it necessary to impose in order to carry out its economic policy. Fully enforced and carried through, the law would have involved centralized allocation of individuals to occupations. This conflicted so sharply with personal liberty that it was enforced in a negligible number of cases and then repealed after the law had been in effect for only a short period. Its repeal ushered in a decided shift in economic policy, marked by reduced reliance on centralized "plans" and "programs" by the dismantling of many controls, and by increased emphasis on the private market. A similar shift in policy occurred in most other democratic countries.

The proximate explanation of these shifts in policy is the limited success of central planning or its outright failure to achieve stated objectives. However, this failure is itself to be attributed, at least in some measure, to the political implications of central planning and to an unwillingness to follow out its logic when doing so requires trampling roughshod on treasured private rights. It may well be that the shift is only a temporary interruption in the collectivist trend of this century. Even so, it illustrates the close relation between political freedom and economic arrangements.

Historical evidence by itself can never be convincing. Perhaps it was sheer coincidence that the expansion of freedom occurred at the same time as the development of capitalist and market institutions. Why should there be a connection? What are the logical links between economic and political freedom? In discussing these questions we shall consider first the market as a direct component of freedom and then the indirect relation between market arrangements and political freedom. A by-product will be an outline of the ideal economic arrangements for a free society.

As liberals we take freedom of the individual, or perhaps the family, as our ultimate goal in judging social arrangements. Freedom as a value in this sense has to do with the interrelations among people; it has no meaning whatsoever to a Robinson Crusoe on an isolated island (without his Man Friday). Robinson Crusoe on his island is subject to "constraint," he has limited "power," and he has only a limited number of alternatives, but there is no problem of freedom in the sense that is relevant to our discussion. Similarly in a society freedom has nothing to say about what an individual does with his freedom; it is not an all-embracing ethic. Indeed, a major aim of the liberal is to leave the ethical problem for the individual to wrestle with. The "really" important ethical problems are those that face an individual in a free society—what he should do with his freedom. There are thus two sets of values that a liberal will emphasize: the values that are relevant to relations among people, the context in which he assigns first priority to freedom, and the values that are relevant to the individual in the exercise of his freedom, the realm of individual ethics and philosophy.

The liberal conceives of men as imperfect beings. He regards the problem of social organization to be as much a negative problem of preventing "bad" people from doing harm as of enabling "good" people to be good; of course, "bad" and "good" people may be the same people, depending on who is judging them.

The basic problem of social organization is how to coordinate the economic activities of large numbers of people. Even in relatively backward societies, extensive division of labor and specialization of function are required to make effective use of available resources. In advanced societies, the scale on which coordination is needed, to take full advantage of the opportunities offered by modern science and technology, is enormously greater. Literally millions of people are involved in providing one another with their daily bread, let alone with their yearly automobiles. The challenge to the believer in liberty is to reconcile this widespread interdependence with individual freedom.

Fundamentally, there are only two ways of coordinating the economic activities of millions. One is central direction involving the use of coercion: the technique of the army and of the modern totalitarian state. The other is voluntary cooperation of individuals: the technique of the marketplace.

The possibility of coordination through voluntary cooperation rests on the elementary—yet frequently denied—proposition that both parties to an economic transaction benefit from it, *provided the transaction is bilaterally voluntary and informed.*

Exchange can therefore bring about coordination without coercion. A working model of a society organized through voluntary exchange is a *free private enterprise exchange economy*—what we have been calling competitive capitalism.

In its simplest form such a society consists of a number of independent households—a collection of Robinson Crusoes, as it were. Each household uses the resources it controls to produce goods and services that it exchanges for goods and services produced by other households on terms mutually acceptable to the two parties to the bargain. It is thereby enabled to satisfy its wants indirectly by producing goods and services for others, rather than directly by producing goods for its own immediate use. The incentive for adopting this indirect route is, of course, the increased product made possible by division of labor and specialization of function. Since the household always has the alternative of producing directly for itself, it need not enter into any exchange unless it benefits from it. Hence no exchange will take place unless both parties do benefit from it. Cooperation is thereby achieved without coercion.

Specialization of function and division of labor would not go far if the ultimate productive unit were the household. In a modern society, we have gone much further. We have introduced enterprises that are intermediaries between individuals in their capacities as suppliers of service and as purchasers of goods. And, similarly, specialization of function and division of labor could not go very far if we had to continue to rely on the barter of product for product. In consequence, money has been introduced as a means of facilitating exchange and of enabling the acts of purchase and of sale to be separated into two parts.

Despite the important role of enterprises and of money in our actual economy, and despite the numerous and complex problems they raise, the central characteristic of the market technique of achieving coordination is fully displayed in the simple exchange economy that contains neither enterprises nor money. As in that simple model, so in the complex enterprise and money-exchange economy cooperation is strictly individual and voluntary *provided* (a) that enterprises are private, so that the ultimate contracting parties are individuals and (b) that individuals are effectively free to enter or not to enter into any particular exchange, so that every transaction is strictly voluntary.

It is far easier to state these provisos in general terms than to spell them out in detail or to specify precisely the institutional arrangements most conducive to their maintenance. Indeed, much of technical economic literature is concerned with precisely these questions. The basic requisite is the maintenance of law and order to prevent physical coercion of one individual by another and to enforce contracts voluntarily entered into, thus giving substance to "private." Aside from this, perhaps the most difficult problems arise from monopoly, which inhibits effective freedom by denying individuals alternatives to the particular exchange, and from "neighborhood effects," effects on third parties for which it is not feasible to charge or recompense them.

As long as effective freedom of exchange is maintained, the central feature of the market organization of economic activity is that it prevents one person from interfering with another in respect of most of his activities. The consumer is protected from coercion by the seller because of the presence of other sellers with whom he can deal. The seller is protected from coercion by the consumer because of other consumers to whom he can sell. The employee is protected from coercion by the employer because of other employers for whom he can work and so on. And the market does this impersonally and without centralized authority.

Indeed a major source of objection to a free economy is precisely that it does this task so well. It gives people what they want instead of what a particular group thinks they ought to want. Underlying most arguments against the free market is a lack of belief in freedom itself.

The existence of a free market does not of course eliminate the need for government. On the contrary government is essential both as a forum for determining the "rules of the game" and as an umpire to interpret and enforce the decided-on rules. What the market does is to reduce greatly the range of issues that must be decided through political means and thereby minimize the extent to which government need participate directly in the game. The characteristic feature of action through political channels is that it tends to require or enforce substantial conformity. The great advantage of the market, on the other hand, is that it permits wide diversity. It is, in political terms, a system of proportional representation. Each man can vote, as it were, for the color of tie he wants and get it; he does not have to see what color the majority wants and then, if he is in the minority, submit.

It is this feature of the market that we refer to when we say that the market provides economic freedom. But this characteristic also has implications that go far beyond the narrowly economic. Political freedom means the absence of coercion of a man by his fellow men. The fundamental threat to freedom is power to coerce, be it in the hands of a monarch, a dictator, an oligarchy, or a momentary majority. The preservation of freedom requires the elimination of such concentration of power to the fullest possible extent and the dispersal and distribution of whatever power cannot be eliminated—a system of checks and balances. By removing the organization of economic activity from the control of political authority, the market eliminates this source of coercive power. It enables economic strength to be a check to political power rather than a reinforcement of it.

Economic power can be widely dispersed. There is no law of conservation that forces the growth of new centers of economic strength at the expense of existing centers. Political power, on the other hand, is more difficult to decentralize. There can be numerous small independent governments. But it is far more difficult to maintain numerous equipotent small centers of political power in a single large government than it is to have numerous centers of economic strength in a single large economy. There can be many millionaires in one large economy. But can there be more than one really outstanding leader, one person on whom the energies and enthusiasms of his countrymen are centered? If the central government gains power, it is likely to be at the expense of local governments. There seems to be something like a fixed total of political power to be distributed. Consequently, if economic power is joined to political power, concentration seems almost inevitable. On the other hand, if economic power is kept in separate hands from political power, it can serve as a check and a counter to political power.

The force of this abstract argument can perhaps best be demonstrated by example. Let us consider first a hypothetical example that may help to bring out the principles involved and then some actual examples from recent experience that illustrate the way in which the market works to preserve political freedom.

One feature of a free society is surely the freedom of individuals to advocate and propagandize openly for a radical change in the structure of the society—so long as the advocacy is restricted to persuasion and does not include force or other forms of coercion. It is a mark of the political freedom of a capitalist society that men can openly advocate and work for socialism. Equally political freedom in a socialist society would require that men be free to advocate the introduction of capitalism. How could the freedom to advocate capitalism be preserved and protected in a socialist society?

In order for men to advocate anything, they must in the first place be able to earn a living. This already raises a problem in a socialist society since all jobs are under the direct control of political authorities. It would take an act of self-denial . . . for a socialist government to permit its employees to advocate policies directly contrary to official doctrine.

But let us suppose this act of self-denial to be achieved. For advocacy of capitalism to mean anything, the proponents must be able to finance their cause: to hold public meetings, publish pamphlets, buy radio time, issue newspapers and magazines, and so on. How could they raise the funds? There might and probably would be men in the socialist society with large incomes, perhaps even large capital sums in the form of government bonds and the like, but these would of necessity be high public officials. It is possible to conceive of a minor socialist official retaining his job although openly advocating capitalism, but it strains credulity to imagine the socialist top brass financing such "subversive" activities.

The only recourse for funds would be to raise small amounts from a large number of minor officials. But this is no real answer. To tap these sources, many people would already have to be persuaded, and our whole problem is how to initiate and finance a campaign to do so. Radical movements in capitalist societies have never been financed this way. They have typically been supported by a few wealthy individuals who have become persuaded—by a Frederick Vanderbilt Field or an Anita McCormick Blaine or a Corliss Lamont, to mention a few names recently prominent, or by a Friedrich Engels, to go farther back. This is a role of inequality of wealth in preserving political freedom that is seldom noted: the role of the patron.

In a capitalist society it is only necessary to convince a few wealthy people to get funds to launch any idea, however strange, and there are many such persons, many independent foci of support. And, indeed, it is not even necessary to persuade people or financial institutions with available funds of the soundness of the ideas to be propagated. It is only necessary to persuade them that the propagation can be financially successful, that the newspaper or magazine or book or other venture will be profitable. The competitive publisher, for example, cannot afford to publish only writing with which he personally agrees; his touchstone must be the likelihood that the market will be large enough to yield a satisfactory return on his investment.

In this way, the market breaks the vicious circle and makes it possible ultimately to finance such ventures by small amounts from many people without first persuading them. There are no such possibilities in the socialist society; there is only the all-powerful state.

Let us stretch our imagination and suppose that a socialist government is aware of this problem and is composed of people anxious to preserve freedom. Could it provide the funds? Perhaps, but it is difficult to see how. It could establish a bureau for subsidizing subversive propaganda. But how could it choose whom to support? If it gave to all who asked, it would shortly find itself out of funds, for socialism cannot repeal the elementary economic law that a sufficiently high price will call forth a large supply. Make the advocacy of radical causes sufficiently remunerative, and the supply of advocates will be unlimited.

Moreover, freedom to advocate unpopular causes does not require that such advocacy be without cost. On the contrary, no society could be stable if advocacy of radical change were costless, much less subsidized. It is entirely appropriate that men make sacrifices to advocate causes in which they deeply believe. Indeed, it is important to preserve freedom only for those people who are willing to practice self-denial, for otherwise freedom degenerates into license and irresponsibility. What is essential is that the cost of advocating unpopular causes be tolerable and not prohibitive.

But we are not yet through. In a free market society, it is enough to have the funds. The suppliers of paper are as willing to sell it to the *Daily Worker* as to the *Wall Street Journal*. In a socialist society, it would not be enough to have the funds. The hypothetical supporter of capitalism would have to persuade a government factory making paper to sell to him, the government printing press to print his pamphlets, a government post office to distribute them among the people, a government agency to rent him a hall in which to talk, and so on.

Perhaps there is some way in which one could overcome these difficulties and preserve freedom in a socialist society. One cannot say it is utterly impossible. What is clear, however, is that there are very real difficulties in establishing institutions that will effectively preserve the possibility of dissent. As far as I know, none of the people who have been in favor of socialism and also in favor of freedom has really faced up to this issue or made even a respectable start at developing the institutional arrangements that would permit freedom under socialism. By contrast it is clear how a free market capitalist society fosters freedom.

A striking practical example of these abstract principles is the experience of Winston Churchill. From 1933 to the outbreak of World War II, Churchill was not permitted to talk over the British radio, which was, of course, a government monopoly administered by the British Broadcasting Corporation (BBC). Here was a leading citizen of his country, a member of Parliament, a former cabinet minister, a man who was desperately trying by every device possible to persuade his countrymen to take steps to ward off the menace of Hitler's Germany. He was not permitted to talk over the radio to the British people because the BBC was a government monopoly and his position was too "controversial."

Another striking example, reported in the January 26, 1959, issue of *Time,* has to do with the "Blacklist Fadeout." Says the *Time* story,

> The Oscar awarding ritual is Hollywood's biggest pitch for dignity, but two years ago dignity suffered. When one Robert Rich was

announced as top writer for the *The Brave One,* he never stepped forward. Robert Rich was a pseudonym, masking one of about 150 writers . . . blacklisted by the industry since 1947 as suspected Communists or fellow travelers. The case was particularly embarrassing because the Motion Picture Academy had barred any Communist or Fifth Amendment pleader from Oscar competition. Last week both the Communist rule and the mystery of Rich's identity were suddenly rescripted.

Rich turned out to be Dalton (*Johnny Got His Gun*) Trumbo, one of the original "Hollywood Ten" writers who refused to testify at the 1947 hearings on Communism in the movie industry. Said producer Frank King, who had stoutly insisted that Robert Rich was "a young guy in Spain with a beard": "We have an obligation to our stockholders to buy the best script we can. Trumbo brought us *The Brave One* and we bought it". . . .

In effect it was the formal end of the Hollywood black list. For barred writers, the informal end came long ago. At least 15% of current Hollywood films are reportedly written by blacklist members. Said Producer King, "There are more ghosts in Hollywood than in Forest Lawn. Every company in town has used the work of blacklisted people. We're just the first to confirm what everybody knows."

One may believe, as I do, that communism would destroy all of our freedoms, that one may be opposed to it as firmly and as strongly as possible and yet, at the same time, also believe that in a free society it is intolerable for a man to be prevented from making voluntary arrangements with others that are mutually attractive because he believes in or is trying to promote communism. His freedom includes his freedom to promote communism. Freedom also, of course, includes the freedom of others not to deal with him under those circumstances. The Hollywood blacklist was an unfree act that destroys freedom because it was a collusive arrangement that used coercive means to prevent voluntary exchanges. It didn't work precisely because the market made it costly for people to preserve the blacklist. The commercial emphasis, the fact that people who are running enterprises have an incentive to make as much money as they can, protected the freedom of the individuals who were blacklisted by providing them with an alternative form of employment and by giving people an incentive to employ them.

If Hollywood and the movie industry had been government enterprises or if in England it had been a question of employment by the British Broadcasting Corporation, it is difficult to believe that the "Hollywood Ten" or their equivalent would have found employment. Equally it is difficult to believe that, under those circumstances, strong proponents of individualism and private enterprise—or indeed strong proponents of any view other than the status quo—would be able to get employment.

Another example of the role of the market in preserving political freedom was revealed in our experience with McCarthyism. Entirely aside from the substantive issues involved and the merits of the charges made, what protection did individuals, in particular government employees, have against irresponsible accusations and probes into matters that it went against their conscience to reveal? Their appeal to the Fifth Amendment would have been a hollow mockery without an alternative to government employment.

Their fundamental protection was the existence of a private market economy in which they could earn a living. Here again the protection was not absolute. Many potential private employers were, rightly or wrongly, averse to hiring those pilloried. It may well be that there was far less justification for the costs imposed on many of the people involved than for the costs generally imposed on people who advocate unpopular causes. But the important point is that the costs were limited and not prohibitive, as they would have been if government employment had been the only possibility.

It is of interest to note that a disproportionately large fraction of the people involved apparently went into the most competitive sectors of the economy—small businesses, trade, running farms—where the market approaches most closely the ideal free market. No one who buys bread knows whether the wheat from which it is made was grown by a Communist or a Republican, by a constitutionalist or a Fascist, or, for that matter, by a Negro or a white. This illustrates how an impersonal market separates economic activities from political views and protects men from being discriminated against in their economic activities for reasons that are irrelevant to their productivity, whether these reasons are associated with their views or their color.

As this example suggests, the groups in our society that have the most at stake in preservating and strengthening competitive capitalism are those minority groups that can most easily become the object of the distrust and enmity of the majority: the Negroes, the Jews, the foreign born, to mention only the most obvious. Yet, paradoxically enough, the enemies of the free market—the Socialists and Communists—have been recruited in disproportionate measure from these groups. Instead of recognizing that the existence of the market has protected them from the attitudes of their fellow countrymen, they mistakenly attribute the residual discrimination to the market.

Note

From the preface, p. xi: "Chapter 1 is a revision of material published earlier under the title used for this book in Felix Morley (ed.), *Essays in Individuality* (University of Pennsylvania Press, 1958) and in still a different form under the same title in *The New Individualist Review*, vol. 1, no. 1 (April 1961).

THREE

THE ROLE OF GOVERNMENT IN A FREE SOCIETY

(1962)

A common objection to totalitarian societies is that they regard the end as justifying the means. Taken literally, this objection is clearly illogical. If the end does not justify the means, what does? But this easy answer does not dispose of the objection; it simply shows that the objection is not well put. To deny that the end justifies the means is indirectly to assert that the end in question is not the ultimate end, that the ultimate end is itself the use of the proper means. Desirable or not, any end that can be attained only by the use of bad means must give way to the more basic end of the use of acceptable means.

To the liberal, the appropriate means are free discussion and voluntary cooperation, which implies that any form of coercion is inappropriate. The ideal is unanimity among responsible individuals achieved on the basis of free and full discussion. This is another way of expressing the goal of freedom.

From this standpoint, the role of the market, as already noted, is that it permits unanimity without conformity; that it is a system of effectively proportional representation. On the other hand, the characteristic feature of action through explicitly political channels is that it tends to require or to enforce substantial conformity. The typical issue must be decided yes or no; at most, provision can be made for a fairly limited number of alternatives. Even the use of proportional representation in its explicitly political form does not alter this conclusion. The number of separate groups that can in fact be represented is narrowly limited, enormously so by comparison with the proportional representation of the market. More important, the fact that the final outcome generally must be a law applicable to all groups, rather than separate legislative enactments for each party represented, means that proportional representation in its political version, far from permitting unanimity without conformity, tends toward ineffectiveness and fragmentation. It thereby operates to destroy any consensus on which unanimity with conformity can rest.

There are clearly some matters with respect to which effective proportional representation is impossible. I cannot get the amount of national defense I want when you want a different amount. With respect to such indivisible matters we can discuss, argue, and vote. But having decided, we must conform. It is precisely the existence of such indivisible matters—protection of the individual and the nation from coercion are clearly the most basic—that prevents exclusive reliance on individual action through the market. If we are to use some of our resources for such indivisible items, we must employ political channels to reconcile differences.

The use of political channels, while inevitable, tends to strain the social cohesion essential for a stable society. The strain is least if agreement for joint action need be reached only on a limited range of issues on which people in any event have common views. Every extension of the range of issues for which explicit agreement is sought strains further the delicate threads that hold society together. If it goes so far as to touch an issue on which men feel deeply yet differently, it may well disrupt the society.

Fundamental differences in basic values can seldom if ever be resolved at the ballot box; ultimately they can only be decided, though not resolved, by conflict. The religious and civil wars of history are a bloody testament to this judgment.

The widespread use of the market reduces the strain on the social fabric by rendering conformity unnecessary with respect to any activities it encompasses. The wider the range of activities covered by the market, the fewer are the issues on which explicitly political decisions are required and hence on which it is necessary to achieve agreement. In turn, the fewer the issues on which agreement is necessary, the greater is the likelihood of getting agreement while maintaining a free society.

Unanimity is, of course, an ideal. In practice, we can afford neither the time nor the effort that would be required to achieve complete unanimity on every issue. We must perforce accept something less. We are thus led to accept majority rule in one form or another as an expedient. That majority rule is an expedient rather than itself a basic principle is clearly shown by the fact that our willingness to resort to majority rule and the size of the majority we require themselves depend on the seriousness of the issue involved. If the matter is of little moment and the minority has no strong feelings about being overruled, a bare plurality will suffice. On the other hand, if the minority feels strongly about the issue involved, even a bare majority will not do. Few of us would be willing to have issues of free speech, for example, decided by a bare majority. Our legal structure is full of such distinctions among the kinds of issues that require different kinds of majorities. At the extreme are those issues embodied in the Constitution. These are the principles that are so important that we are willing to make minimal concessions to expediency. Something like essential consensus was achieved initially in accepting them; we require something like essential consensus for a change in them.

The self-denying ordinance to refrain from majority rule on certain kinds of issues that is embodied in our Constitution and in similar written or unwritten constitutions elsewhere, and the specific provisions in these constitutions or their equivalents prohibiting coercion of individuals, are themselves to be regarded as reached by free discussion and as reflecting essential unanimity about means.

I turn now to consider more specifically, though still in very broad terms, what the areas are that cannot be handled through the market at all or can be handled only at so great a cost that the use of political channels may be preferable.

Government as Rule Maker and Umpire

It is important to distinguish the day-to-day activities of people from the general customary and legal framework within which these take place. The day-to-day activities are like the actions of the participants in a game when they are playing it; the framework, like the rules of the game they play. And just as a good game requires acceptance by the players both of the rules and of the umpire to interpret and enforce them, so a good society requires that its members agree on the general conditions that will govern relations among them, on some means of arbitrating different interpretations of these conditions, and on some device for enforcing compliance with the generally accepted rules. As in games, so also in society, most of the general conditions are the unintended outcome of custom, accepted unthinkingly. At most, we consider explicitly only minor modifications in them, though the cumulative effect of a series of minor modifications may be a drastic alteration in the character of the game or of the society. In both games and society, no set of rules can prevail unless most participants most of the time conform to them without external sanctions, unless there is a broad underlying social consensus.

But we cannot rely on custom or on this consensus alone to interpret and to enforce the rules; we need an umpire. These then
are the basic roles of government in a free society: to provide a
means whereby we can modify the rules, to mediate differences
among us on the meaning of the rules, and to enforce compliance
with the rules on the part of those few who would otherwise not
play the game.

The need for government in these respects arises because absolute freedom is impossible. However attractive anarchy may be as
a philosophy, it is not feasible in a world of imperfect men. Men's
freedoms can conflict; when they do, one man's freedom must be
limited to preserve another's, as a Supreme Court Justice once put
it, "My freedom to move my fist must be limited by the proximity
of your chin."

The major problem in deciding the appropriate activities of
government is how to resolve such conflicts among the freedoms
of different individuals. In some cases the answer is easy. There is
little difficulty in attaining near unanimity to the proposition that
one man's freedom to murder his neighbor must be sacrificed to
preserve the freedom of the other man to live. In other cases, the
answer is difficult. In the economic area, a major problem arises
in respect of the conflict between freedom to combine and freedom to compete. What meaning is to be attributed to *free* as modi-
fying *enterprise*? In the United States, *free* has been understood to
mean that anyone is free to set up an enterprise, which means that
existing enterprises are not free to keep out competitors except by
selling a better product at the same price or the same product at
a lower price. In the continental tradition, on the other hand, the
meaning has generally been that enterprises are free to do what
they want, including the fixing of prices, the division of markets,
and the adoption of other techniques to keep out potential competitors. Perhaps the most difficult specific problem in this area
arises with respect to combinations among laborers, where the

problem of freedom to combine and freedom to compete is particularly acute.

A still more basic economic area in which the answer is both difficult and important is the definition of property rights. The notion of property, as it has developed over centuries and as it is embodied in our legal codes, has become so much a part of us that we tend to take it for granted and fail to recognize the extent to just what constitutes property and what rights the ownership of property confers are complex social creations rather than self-evident propositions. Does my having title to land, for example, and my freedom to use my property as I wish, permit me to deny to someone else the right to fly over my land in his airplane? Or does his right to use his airplane take precedence? Or does this depend on how high he flies? Or how much noise he makes? Does voluntary exchange require that he pay me for the privilege of flying over my land? Or that I must pay him to refrain from flying over it? The mere mention of royalties, copyrights, patents, shares of stock in corporations, riparian rights, and the like may perhaps emphasize the role of generally accepted social rules in the very definition of property. It may suggest also that, in many cases, the existence of a well specified and generally accepted definition of property is far more important than just what the definition is.

Another economic area that raises particularly difficult problems is the monetary system. Government responsibility for the monetary system has long been recognized. It is explicitly provided for in the constitutional provision that gives Congress the power "to coin money, regulate the value thereof, and of foreign coin." There is probably no other area of economic activity with respect to which government action has been so uniformly accepted. This habitual and by now almost unthinking acceptance of governmental responsibility makes thoroughly understanding the grounds for such responsibility all the more necessary since it enhances the danger that the scope of government will spread from activities that are, to those that are not, appropriate in a free society, from providing a monetary framework to determining the allocation of resources among individuals.

In summary, the organization of economic activity through voluntary exchange presumes that we have provided, through government, for the maintenance of law and order to prevent coercion of one individual by another, the enforcement of contracts voluntarily entered into, the definition of the meaning of property rights, the interpretation and enforcement of such rights, and the provision of a monetary framework.

Action through Government on Grounds of Technical Monopoly and Neighborhood Effects

The role of government just considered is to do something that the market cannot do for itself, namely, to determine, arbitrate, and enforce the rules of the game. We may also want to do through government some things that might conceivably be done through the market but that technical or similar conditions render difficult. These all reduce to cases in which strictly voluntary exchange is either exceedingly costly or practically impossible. There are two general classes of such cases: monopoly and similar market imperfections and neighborhood effects.

Exchange is truly voluntary only when nearly equivalent alternatives exist. Monopoly implies the absence of alternatives and thereby inhibits effective freedom of exchange. In practice monopoly frequently, if not generally, arises from government support or from collusive agreements among individuals. With respect to these, the problem is either to avoid governmental fostering of monopoly or to stimulate the effective enforcement of rules such as those embodied in our antitrust laws. However, monopoly may also arise because it is technically efficient to have a single producer or enterprise. I venture to suggest that such cases are more limited than is supposed, but they unquestionably do arise. A simple example is perhaps the provision of telephone services within a community. I shall refer to such cases as a "technical" monopoly.

When technical conditions make a monopoly the natural outcome of competitive market forces, there are only three alternatives that seem available: private monopoly, public monopoly, or public regulation. All three are bad so we must choose among evils. Henry Simons, observing public regulation of monopoly in the United States, found the results so distasteful that he concluded public monopoly would be a lesser evil. Walter Eucken, a noted German liberal, observing public monopoly in German railroads, found the results so distasteful that he concluded public regulation would be a lesser evil. Having learned from both, I reluctantly conclude that, if tolerable, private monopoly may be the least of the evils.

If society were static so that the conditions that give rise to a technical monopoly were sure to remain, I would have little confidence in this solution. In a rapidly changing society, however, the conditions making for a technical monopoly frequently change, and I suspect that both public regulation and public monopoly are likely to be less responsive to such changes in conditions, to be less readily capable of elimination, than private monopoly.

Railroads in the United States are an excellent example. A large degree of monopoly in railroads was perhaps inevitable on technical grounds in the nineteenth century. This was the justification for the Interstate Commerce Commission (ICC). But conditions have changed. The emergence of road and air transport has reduced the monopoly element in railroads to negligible proportions. Yet we have not eliminated the ICC. On the contrary, the ICC, which started out as an agency to protect the public from exploitation by the railroads, has become an agency to protect railroads from competition by trucks and other means of transport and, more recently, even to protect existing truck companies from competition by new entrants. Similarly in England when the railroads were nationalized, trucking was at first brought into the state monopoly. If railroads had never been subjected to regulation in the United States, it is nearly certain that by now transportation, including railroads, would be a highly competitive industry with little or no remaining monopoly elements.

The choice between the evils of private monopoly, public monopoly, and public regulation cannot, however, be made once and for all, independently of the factual circumstances. If the technical monopoly is of a service or commodity that is regarded as essential and if its monopoly power is sizable, even the short-run effects of private unregulated monopoly may not be tolerable and either public regulation or ownership may be a lesser evil.

Technical monopoly may on occasion justify a de facto public monopoly. It cannot by itself justify a public monopoly achieved by making it illegal for anyone else to compete. For example, there is no way to justify our present public monopoly of the post office. It may be argued that the carrying of mail is a technical monopoly and that a government monopoly is the least of evils. Along these lines one could perhaps justify a government post office but not the present law, which makes it illegal for anybody else to carry mail. If the delivery of mail is a technical monopoly, no one will be able to succeed in competition with the government. If it is not, there is no reason why the government should be engaged in it. The only way to find out is to leave other people free to enter.

The historical reason we have a post office monopoly is because the Pony Express did such a good job of carrying the mail across the continent that, when the government introduced transcontinental service, it couldn't compete effectively and lost money. The result was a law making it illegal for anybody else to carry the mail. That is why the Adams Express Company is an investment trust today instead of an operating company. I conjecture that if entry into the mail-carrying business were open to all, there would be a large number of firms entering it and that this archaic industry would become revolutionized in short order.

A second general class of cases in which strictly voluntary exchange is impossible arises when actions of individuals have effects on other individuals for which it is not feasible to charge or recompense them. This is the problem of "neighborhood effects." An obvious example is the pollution of a stream. The man who pollutes a stream is in effect forcing others to exchange good water for bad. These others might be willing to make the exchange at a price. But it is not feasible for them, acting individually, to avoid the exchange or to enforce appropriate compensation.

A less obvious example is the provision of highways. In this case, it is technically possible to identify and hence charge individuals for their use of the roads and so to have private operation. However, for general access roads, involving many points of entry and exit, the costs of collection would be extremely high if a charge were to be made for the specific services received by each individual because of the necessity of establishing tollbooths or the equivalent at all entrances. The gasoline tax is a much cheaper method of charging individuals roughly in proportion to their use of the roads. This method, however, is one in which the particular payment cannot be identified closely with the particular use. Hence, it is hardly feasible to have private enterprise provide the service and collect the charge without establishing an extensive private monopoly.

These considerations do not apply to long-distance turnpikes with a high density of traffic and limited access. For these the costs of collection are small and in many cases are now being paid, and there are often numerous alternatives so that there is no serious monopoly problem. Hence there is every reason why these should be privately owned and operated. If so owned and operated, the enterprise running the highway should receive the gasoline taxes paid on account of travel on it.

Parks are an interesting example because they illustrate the difference between cases that can and cases that cannot be justified by neighborhood effects because almost everyone at first sight regards the conduct of national parks as obviously a valid function of government. In fact, however, neighborhood effects may justify a city park; they do not justify a national park, such as Yellowstone National Park or the Grand Canyon. What is the fundamental difference between the two? For the city park, it is extremely difficult to identify the people who benefit from it and to charge them for the benefits that they receive. If there is a park in the middle of the city, the houses on all sides get the benefit of the open space, and people who walk through it or by it also benefit. To maintain toll collectors at the gates or to impose annual charges per window overlooking the park would be very expensive and difficult. The entrances to a national park like Yellowstone, on the other hand, are few; most of the people who come stay for a considerable period of time, and it is perfectly feasible to set up toll gates and collect admission charges. This is indeed now done, though the charges do not cover the whole costs. If the public wants this kind of an activity enough to pay for it, private enterprises will have every incentive to provide such parks. And, of course, there are many private enterprises of this nature now in existence. I cannot myself conjure up any neighborhood effects or important monopoly effects that would justify governmental activity in this area.

Considerations like those I have treated under the heading of neighborhood effects have been used to rationalize almost every conceivable intervention. In many instances, however, this rationalization is special pleading rather than a legitimate application of the concept of neighborhood effects. Neighborhood effects cut both ways. They can be a reason for limiting the activities of government as well as for expanding them. Neighborhood effects impede voluntary exchange because it is difficult to identify the effects on third parties and to measure their magnitude, but this difficulty is present in governmental activity as well. It is hard to know when neighborhood effects are sufficiently large to justify particular costs in overcoming them and even harder to distribute the costs in an appropriate fashion. Consequently when government engages in activities to overcome neighborhood effects, it will in part introduce an additional set of neighborhood effects by failing to charge or to compensate individuals properly. Whether the original or the new neighborhood effects are the more serious can only be judged by the facts of the individual case and, even then, only very approximately. Furthermore the use of government to overcome neighborhood effects itself has an extremely important neighborhood effect which is unrelated to the particular occasion for government action. Every act of government intervention limits the area of individual freedom directly and threatens the preservation of freedom indirectly.

Our principles offer no hard and fast line on how far it is appropriate to use government to accomplish jointly what it is difficult or impossible for us to accomplish separately through strictly voluntary exchange. In any particular case of proposed intervention, we must make up a balance sheet, listing separately the advantages and disadvantages. Our principles tell us what items to put on the one side and what items on the other and thus give us some basis for attaching importance to the different items. In particular, we shall always want to enter on the liability side of any proposed government intervention its neighborhood effect in threatening freedom and give this effect considerable weight. Just how much weight to give to it, as to other items, depends upon the circumstances. If, for example, existing government intervention is minor, we shall attach a smaller weight to the negative effects of additional government intervention. This is an important reason why many earlier liberals, like Henry Simons, writing at a time when government was small by today's standards, were willing to have government undertake activities that today's liberal would not accept now that government has become so overgrown.

Action through Government on Paternalistic Grounds

Freedom is a tenable objective only for responsible individuals. We do not believe in freedom for madmen or children. The necessity of drawing a line between responsible individuals and others is inescapable, yet it means that there is an essential ambiguity in our ultimate objective of freedom. Paternalism is inescapable for those whom we designate as not responsible.

The clearest case, perhaps, is that of madmen. We are willing neither to permit them freedom nor to shoot them. It would be nice if we could rely on voluntary activities of individuals to house and care for the madmen. But I think we cannot rule out the possibility that such charitable activities will be inadequate if only because of the neighborhood effect involved in the fact that I benefit if another man contributes to the care of the insane. For this reason we may be willing to arrange for their care through government.

Children offer a more difficult case. The ultimate operative unit in our society is the family, not the individual. Yet the acceptance of the family as the unit rests in considerable part on expediency rather than principle. We believe that parents are generally best able to protect their children and to provide for their development into responsible individuals for whom freedom is appropriate. But we do not believe in the freedom of parents to do what they will with other people. The children are responsible individuals in embryo, and a believer in freedom believes in protecting their ultimate rights.

To put this in a different and what may seem a more callous way, children are at one and the same time consumer goods and potentially responsible members of society. The freedom of individuals to use their economic resources as they want includes the freedom to use them to have children—to buy, as it were, the services of children as a particular form of consumption. But once this choice is exercised, the children have a value in and of themselves and have a freedom of their own that is not simply an extension of the freedom of the parents.

The paternalistic ground for governmental activity is in many ways the most troublesome to a liberal, for it involves the acceptance of a principle—that some shall decide for others—that he finds objectionable in most applications and that he rightly regards as a hallmark of his chief intellectual opponents: the proponents of collectivism in one or another of its guises, whether it be communism, socialism, or a welfare state. Yet there is no use pretending that problems are simpler than in fact they are. There is no avoiding the need for some measure of paternalism. As Dicey wrote in 1914 about an act for the protection of mental defectives, "the Mental Deficiency Act is the first step along a path on which no sane man can decline to enter, but which, if too far pursued, will bring statesmen across difficulties hard to meet without considerable interference with individual liberty."[1] There is no formula that can tell us where to stop. We must rely on our fallible judgment and, having reached a judgment, on our ability to persuade our fellow men that it is a correct judgment, or their ability to persuade us to modify our views. We must put our faith, here as elsewhere, in a consensus reached by imperfect and biased men through free discussion and trial and error.

Conclusion

A government that maintained law and order, defined property rights, served as a means whereby we could modify property rights and other rules of the economic game, adjudicated disputes about the interpretation of the rules, enforced contracts, promoted competition, provided a monetary framework, engaged in activities to counter technical monopolies and to overcome neighborhood effects widely regarded as sufficiently important to justify government intervention, and that supplemented private charity and the private family in protecting the irresponsible, whether madman or child, such a government would clearly have important functions to perform. The consistent liberal is not an anarchist.

Yet it is also true that such a government would have clearly limited functions and would refrain from a host of activities that are now undertaken by federal and state government in the United States and their counterparts in other Western countries . . . it may help to give a sense of proportion about the role that a liberal would assign government simply to list, in closing this chapter, some activities currently undertaken by government in the United States that cannot, so far as I can see, validly be justified in terms of the principles outlined above:

1. Parity price support programs for agriculture.
2. Tariffs on imports or restrictions on exports, such as current oil import quotas, sugar quotas, and so on.
3. Governmental control of output, such as through the farm program or through pro-rationing of oil as is done by the Texas Railroad Commission.
4. Rent control, such as is still practiced in New York, or more general price and wage controls such as were imposed during and just after World War II.
5. Legal minimum wage rates, or legal maximum prices, such as the legal maximum of zero on the rate of interest that can be paid on demand deposits by commercial banks or the legally fixed maximum rates that can be paid on savings and time deposits.

6. Detailed regulation of industries, such as the regulation of transportation by the Interstate Commerce Commission, which had some justification on technical monopoly grounds when initially introduced for railroads; it has none now for any means of transport. Another example is detailed regulation of banking.

7. A similar example, but one which deserves special mention because of its implicit censorship and violation of free speech, is the control of radio and television by the Federal Communications Commission.

8. Present Social Security programs, especially the old-age and retirement programs compelling people in effect (a) to spend a specified fraction of their income on the purchase of a retirement annuity and (b) to buy the annuity from a publicly operated enterprise.

9. Licensure provisions in various cities and states that restrict particular enterprises or occupations or professions to people who have a license, where the license is more than a receipt for a tax which anyone who wished to enter the activity may pay.

10. So-called public-housing and the host of other subsidy programs directed at fostering residential construction such as the Federal Housing Administration and the Veterans' Administration's guarantee of mortgage and the like.

11. Conscription to man the military services in peacetime. The appropriate free market arrangement is volunteer military forces, which is to say hiring men to serve. There is no justification for not paying whatever price is necessary to attract the required number of men. Present arrangements are inequitable and arbitrary, seriously interfere with the freedom of young men to shape their lives, and probably are even more costly than the market

alternative. (Universal military training to provide a reserve for wartime is a different problem and may be justified on liberal grounds.)

12. National parks, as noted above.
13. The legal prohibition on the carrying of mail for profit.
14. Publicly owned and operated toll roads, as noted above.

This list is far from comprehensive.

Note

1. A. V. Dicey, *Lectures on the Relation between Law and Public Opinion in England during the Nineteenth Century* (2d ed., London: Macmillan & Co., 1914), p. li.

FOUR

IS A FREE SOCIETY STABLE?

(1962)

There is a strong tendency for all of us to regard what is as if it were the "natural" or "normal" state of affairs, to lack perspective because of the tyranny of the status quo. It is, therefore, well, from time to time, to make a deliberate effort to look at things in a broader context. In such a context anything approaching a free society is an exceedingly rare event. Only during short intervals in man's recorded history has there been anything approaching what we would call a free society in existence over any appreciable part of the globe. And even during such intervals, as at the moment, the greater part of mankind has lived under regimes that could by no stretch of the imagination be called free.

This casual empirical observation raises the question whether a free society may not be a system in unstable equilibrium. If one were to take a purely historical point of view, one would have to say that the normal, in the sense of average, state of mankind is a state of tyranny and despotism. Perhaps this is the equilibrium state of society that tends to arise in the relation of man to his fellows. Perhaps highly special circumstances must exist to render a free society possible. And perhaps these special circumstances, the existence of which account for the rare episodes of freedom, are themselves by their nature transitory so that the kind of society we all of us believe in is highly unlikely to be maintained even if once attained.

This problem has, of course, been extensively discussed in the literature. In his great book, *Lectures on Law and Public Opinion in the Nineteenth Century,* written at the end of the nineteenth century, A. V. Dicey discusses a very similar question. How was it, he asks, that toward the end of the nineteenth century there seemed to be a shift in English public opinion away from the doctrine of liberalism and toward collectivism, even though, just prior to the shift, individualism and laissez-faire were at something like their high tide, seeming to have captured English public opinion and seeming to be producing the results that their proponents had promised in the form of an expansion of economic activity, a rise in the standard of life, and the like?

As you may recall, Dicey dates the change in public opinion in Britain away from individualism and toward collectivism at about 1870–90. Dicey answers his question by essentially reversing it, saying that in its original form it may be a foolish question. Perhaps the relevant question is not why people turned away from individualism toward collectivism but how they were induced to accept the queer notion of individualism in the first place. The argument for a free society, he goes on to say, is a very subtle and sophisticated argument. At every point, it depends on the indirect rather than the direct effect of the policy followed. If one is concerned to remedy clear evils in a society, as everyone is, the natural reaction is to say, "let us do something about it," with the "us" in this statement in a large number of cases be translated into the "government," so the natural reaction is to pass a law. The argument that maybe the attempt to correct this particular evil by extending the hand of the government will have indirect effects whose aggregate consequences may be far worse than any direct benefits that flow from the action taken is a rather sophisticated argument. And yet this is the kind of argument that underlies a belief in a free or laissez-faire society.

If you look at each evil as it arises, in and of itself, there will almost always tend to be strong pressures to do something about it. This will be so because the direct effects are clear and obvious, while the indirect effects are remote and devious, and because there tends to be a concentrated group of people who have strong interests in favor of a particular measure whereas the opponents, like the indirect effects of the measure, are diffused. One can cite example after example along this line. Indeed I think it is true that most crude fallacies about economic policies derive from neglecting the indirect effects of those policies.

The tariff is one example. The benefits that are alleged to flow from a tariff are clear and obvious. If a tariff is imposed, a specified group of people, whose names can almost be listed, seem to be benefited in the first instance. The harm that is wrought by the tariff is borne by people whose names one does not know and who are unlikely themselves to know that they are or will be harmed. The tariff does most harm to people who have special capacities for producing the exports that would pay for the goods that would be imported in the absence of a tariff. With a tariff in effect, the potential export industry may never exist, and no one will ever know that he might have been employed in it or who would have been. The indirect harm to consumers via a more inefficient allocation of resources and higher prices for the resulting products is spread even more thinly through the society. Thus the case for a tariff seems quite clear on first glance. And this is true in case after case.

This natural tendency to engage in state action in specific instances can, it would seem, and this is Dicey's argument, be offset only by a widespread general acceptance of a philosophy of noninterference, by a general presumption against undertaking any one of a large class of actions. And, says Dicey, what is really amazing and surprising is that for so long a period as a few decades, sufficiently widespread public opinion developed in Britain in favor of the general principle of nonintervention and laissez-faire as to overcome the natural tendency to pass a law for the particular cases. As soon as this general presumption weakened, it meant the emergence of a climate of opinion in favor of specific government intervention.

Dicey's argument is enormously strengthened by an asymmetry between a shift toward individualism and a shift away from it. In the first place, there is what I have called the tyranny of the status quo. Anyone who wants to see how strong that tyranny is can do no better, I believe, than to read Dicey's book now. On reading it he will discover how extreme and extensive a collectivist he is, as judged by the kinds of standards for governmental action that seemed obvious and appropriate to Dicey when he wrote his lectures. In discussing issues of this kind, the tendency always is to take *what is* for granted, to assume that it is perfectly all right and reasonable and that the problem to argue about is the next step. This tends to mean that movements in any one direction are difficult to reverse. A second source of asymmetry is the general dilemma that faces the liberal: tolerance of the intolerant. The belief in individualism includes the belief in tolerating the intolerant. It includes the belief that the society is only worth defending if it is one in which we resort to persuasion rather than to force and in which we defend freedom of discussion on the part of those who would undermine the system itself. If one departs from a free society, the people in power in a collectivist society will not hesitate to use force to keep it from being changed. Under such circumstances it is more difficult to achieve a revolution that would convert a totalitarian or collectivist society into an individualist society than it is to do the reverse. From the point of view of the forces that may work in the direction of rendering a free society an unstable system, this is certainly one of the most important strengths of Dicey's general argument.

Perhaps the most famous argument alleging the instability of a free enterprise or capitalist society is the Marxian. Marx argued that there were inherent historical tendencies within a capitalist society that would tend to lead to its destruction. As you know, he predicted that as it developed, capitalism would produce a division of society into sharp classes, the impoverishment of the masses, the despoilment of the middle classes, and a declining rate of profit. He predicted that the combined result would be a class struggle in which the class of the "expropriated," or the proletarian class, would assume power.

Marx's analysis is at least in part to be regarded as a scientific analysis attempting to derive hypotheses that could be used to predict consequences that were likely to occur. His predictions have uniformly been wrong; none of the major consequences that he predicted has in fact occurred. Instead of a widening split among classes, there has tended to be a reduction of class barriers. Instead of a despoilment of the middle class, there has tended to be, if anything, an increase in the middle class relative to the extremes. Instead of the impoverishment of the masses, there has been the largest rise in the standard of life of the masses that history has ever seen. We must therefore reject his theory as having been disproved.

The lack of validity of Marx's theory does not mean that it has been unimportant. It had the enormous importance of leading many, if not a majority, of the intellectual and ruling classes to regard tendencies of the kind he predicted as inevitable, thereby leading them to interpret what did go on in different terms than they otherwise would. Perhaps the most striking example has been the extent to which intellectuals and people in general have taken it for granted that the development of a capitalist society has meant an increased concentration of industrial power and an increase in the degree of monopoly. Although this view has largely reflected a confusion between changes in absolute size and changes in relative size, in part I think it was produced by the fact that this was something they were told to look for by Marx. I don't mean to attribute this view solely to the Marxian influence. But I think that in this and other instances, the Marxian argument has indirectly affected the patterns of thinking of a great many people, including many who would regard themselves as strongly anti-Marxian. Indeed, in many ways the ideas have been most potent when they have lost their labels. In this way, Marx's ideas had an enormous intellectual importance, even though his scientific analysis and predictions have all been contradicted by experience.

In more recent times, Joseph Schumpeter has offered a more subtle and intellectually more satisfactory defense of essentially the Marxian conclusion. Schumpeter's attitude toward Marx is rather interesting. He demonstrates that Marx was wrong in every separate particular, yet proceeds both to accept the major import of his conclusions and to argue that Marx was a very great man. Whereas Marx's view was that capitalism would destroy itself by its failure, Schumpeter's view was that capitalism would destroy itself by its success. Schumpeter believed that large-scale enterprises and monopolies have real advantages in promoting technological progress and growth and that these advantages would give them a competitive edge in the economic struggle. The success of capitalism would therefore, he argued, be associated with a growth of very large enterprises and with the spread of something like semi-monopoly over the industrial scene. In its turn, he thought that this development would tend to convert businessmen into bureaucrats. Large organizations have much in common whether they are governmental or private. They inevitably, he believed, produced an increasing separation between the ultimate owners of the enterprises and the individuals who were in positions of importance in managing the enterprises. Such individuals are induced to place high values upon technical performance and to become adaptable to a kind of civil service socialist organization of society. In addition, this process would create the kind of skills in the managerial elite that would be necessary in order to have a collectivist or governmentally controlled society. The development of this bureaucratic elite, with its tendency to place greater and greater emphasis on security and stability and to accept centralized control, would tend, he believed, to have the effect of establishing a climate of opinion highly favorable to a shift to an explicitly socialized and centralized state.

The view that Schumpeter expressed has much in common with what Burnham labeled a managerial revolution although the two are not by any means the same. There is also much in common between Schumpeter's analysis and the distinction that Veblen drew in his analysis of the price system between the roles of entrepreneurs and engineers, between "business" and "industry." There are also large differences. Veblen saw the engineer as the productive force in the society, the entrepreneur as the destructive force. Schumpeter, if anything, saw matters the other way. He saw the entrepreneur as the creative force in society and the engineer as simply his handmaiden. But I think there is much in common between the two analyses with respect to the belief that power would tend to shift from the one to the other.

For myself, I must confess that while I find Schumpeter's analysis intriguing and intellectually fascinating, I cannot accept his thesis. It seems to me to reflect in large part a widespread bias that emphasizes the large and few as opposed to the small and numerous, a tendency to see the merits of scale and not to recognize the merits of large numbers of separate people working in diverse activities. In any event, so far as one can judge, there has been no striking tendency in experience toward an increasing concentration of economic activity in large bureaucratic private enterprises. Some enormous enterprises have of course arisen. But there has also been a very rapid growth in small enterprises. What has happened in this country at least is that the large enterprises have tended to be concentrated in communication and manufacturing. These industries have tended to account for a roughly constant proportion of total economic activity. Small enterprises have tended to be concentrated in agriculture and services. Agriculture has declined in importance and in the number of enterprises, while the service industries have grown in both. If one leaves government aside, as Schumpeter's thesis requires one to do, so far as one can judge from the evidence, there seems to have been no particularly consistent tendency for the fraction of economic activity that is carried on in any given percentage of the enterprises to have grown. What has happened is that small enterprises and big enterprises have both grown in scale, so that what we now call a small enterprise may be large by some earlier standard. However, the thesis that Schumpeter developed is certainly sophisticated and subtle and deserves serious attention.

There is another direction, it seems to me, in which there is a different kind of a tendency for capitalism to undermine itself by its own success. The tendency I have in mind can probably best be brought out by the experience of Great Britain, which tends to provide the best laboratory for many of these forces. It has to do with the attitude of the public at large toward law and toward law obedience. Britain has a wide and deserved reputation for the extraordinary obedience of its people to the law. It has not always been so. At the turn of the nineteenth century, and earlier, the British had a very different reputation as a nation of people who would obey no law or almost no law, a nation of smugglers, a nation in which corruption and inefficiency was rife, and in which one could not get very much done through governmental channels.

Indeed, one of the factors that led Bentham and the Utilitarians toward laissez-faire (this is a view that is also expressed by Dicey) was the self-evident truth that if you wanted to get evils corrected, you could not expect to do so through the government of the time. The government was corrupt and inefficient. It was clearly oppressive. It was something that had to be gotten out of the way as a first step to reform. The fundamental philosophy of the Utilitarians or any philosophy that puts its emphasis on some kind of a sum of utilities, however loose may be the expression, does not lead to laissez-faire in principle. It leads to whatever kind of organization of economic activity is thought to produce results that are regarded as good in the sense of adding to the sum total of utilities. I think the major reason the Utilitarians tended to be in favor of laissez-faire was the obvious fact that government was incompetent to perform any of the tasks they wanted to see performed.

Whatever the reason for its appeal, the adoption of laissez-faire had some important consequences. Once laissez-faire was adopted, the economic incentive for corruption was largely removed. After all, if governmental officials had no favors to grant, there was no need to bribe them. And if there was nothing to be gained from government, it could hardly be a source of corruption. Moreover, the laws that were left were for the most part, and again I am oversimplifying and exaggerating, laws that were widely accepted as proper and desirable: laws against theft, robbery, murder, and so on. This is in sharp contrast to a situation in which the legislative structure designates as crimes what people individually do not regard as crimes or makes it illegal for people to do what seems to them the sensible thing. The latter situation tends to reduce respect for the law. One of the unintended and indirect effects of laissez-faire was thus to establish a climate in Britain of a much greater degree of obedience and respect for the law than had existed earlier. Probably there were other forces at work in this development, but I believe that the establishment of laissez-faire laid the groundwork for a reform in the civil service in the latter part of the century—the establishment of a civil service chosen on the basis of examinations and merit and of professional competence. You could get that kind of development because the incentives to seek such places for purposes of exerting improper influence were greatly reduced when government had few favors to confer.

In these ways the development of laissez-faire laid the groundwork for a widespread respect for the law, on the one hand, and a relatively incorrupt, honest, and efficient civil service, on the other, both of which are essential preconditions for the operation of a collectivist society. In order for a collectivist society to operate, the people must obey the laws and there must be a civil service that can and will carry out the laws. The success of capitalism established these preconditions for a movement in the direction of much greater state intervention.

The process I have described obviously runs both ways. A movement in the direction of a collectivist society involves increased governmental intervention into the daily lives of people and the conversion into crimes of actions that are regarded by the ordinary person as entirely proper. These tend in turn to undermine respect for the law and to give incentives to corrupt state officials. There can, I think, be little doubt that this process has begun in Britain and has gone a substantial distance. Although respect for the law may still be greater than it is here, most observers would agree that respect for the law in Britain has gone down decidedly in the course of the last twenty or thirty years, certainly since the war, as a result of the kind of laws people have been asked to obey. On the occasions I have been in England, I have had access to two sources of information that generally yield quite different answers. One is people associated with academic institutions, all of whom are quite shocked at the idea that any British citizen might evade the law, except perhaps for transactions involving exchanging pounds for dollars when exchange control was in effect. It also happens that I had contact with people engaged in small businesses. They tell a rather different story, one that I suspect comes closer to being valid, about the extent to which regulations were honored in the breach and taxes and customs regulations evaded; the one thing that is uniform among people or almost uniform is that nobody or almost nobody has any moral repugnance to smuggling, certainly not when he is smuggling something into some country other than his own.

The erosion of the capital stock of willingness to obey the law reduces the capacity of a society to run a centralized state, to move away from freedom. This effect on law obedience is thus one that is reversible and runs in both directions. It is another major factor that needs to be taken into account in judging the likely stability of a free system in the long run.

I have been emphasizing forces and approaches that are mostly pessimistic in terms of our values in the sense that most of them are reasons why a free society is likely to be unstable and to change into a collectivist system. I should like therefore to turn to some of the tendencies that may operate in the other direction.

What are the sources of strength for a free society that may help to maintain it? One of the major sources of strength is the tendency for extension of economic intervention in a wide range of areas to interfere directly and clearly with political liberty and thus to make people aware of the conflict between the two. This has been the course of events in Great Britain after the war and in many other countries. I need not repeat or dwell on this point.

A second source of strength is one that has already been suggested by my comments on law obedience. In many ways perhaps the major hope for a free society is precisely that feature in a free society tha makes it so efficient and productive in its economic activity, namely, the ingenuity of millions of people, each of whom is trying to further his interests, in part by finding ways to get around state regulation. If I may refer to my own casual observation of Britain and France a few years after the war, the impression that I formed on the the basis of very little evidence but that seemed to me to be supported by further examination was that Britain at the time was being economically strangled by the law obedience of her citizens while France was being saved by the existence of the black market. The price system is a most effective and efficient system for organizing resources. As long as people try to make it operate, it can surmount a lot of problems. There is the famous story about the man who wrote a letter to Adam Smith saying that some policy or other was going to be the ruin of England. And Adam Smith, as I understand the story, wrote back and said, "Young man, there is a lot of ruin in a nation."

This seems to me an important point. Once government embarks on intervention into and regulation of private activities, this establishes an incentive for large numbers of individuals to use their ingenuity to find ways to get around the government regulations. One result is that there appears to be a lot more regulation than there really is. Another is that the time and energy of government officials are increasingly taken up with the need to plug the holes in the regulations that the citizens are finding, creating, and exploiting. From this point of view, Parkinson's Law about the growth of bureaucracy without a corresponding growth of output may be a favorable feature for the maintenance of a free society. An efficient governmental organization, not an inefficient one, is almost surely the greater threat to a free society. One of the virtues of a free society is precisely that the market tends to be a more efficient organizing principle than centralized direction. Centralized direction in this way means always having to fight something of a losing battle.

Very closely related to this point and perhaps only another aspect of it is the difference between the visibility of monopolistic action, whether governmental or private, and of actions through the market. When people are acting through the market, millions of people are engaging in activities in a variety of ways that are highly impersonal, not very well recognized, and almost none of which attracts attention. On the other hand, governmental actions, and this is equally true of actions by private monopolies, whether of labor or industry, tend to be conducted by persons who get into the headlines, to attract notice. I have often conducted the experiment of asking people to list the major industries in the United States. In many ways, the question is a foolish one because there is no clear definition of industry. Yet people have some concept of industry, and the interesting thing is that the result is always very similar. People always list those industries in which there is a high degree of concentration. They list the automobile industry, never the garment industry, although the garment industry is far larger by any economic measure than the automobile industry. I have never had anybody list the industry of providing domestic service, although it employs many more people than the steel industry. Estimates of importance are always biased in the direction of those industries that are monopolized or concentrated and so are in the hands of few firms. Everybody knows the names of the leading producers of automobiles. Few could list the leading producers of men's and women's clothing or of furniture, although these are both very large industries. So competition, working through the market, precisely because it is impersonal, anonymous, and works its way in devious methods, tends to be underestimated in importance; the kinds of personal activities that are associated with government, with monopoly, with trade unions, tend to be exaggerated in importance.

Because this kind of direct personal activity by large organizations, whether governmental or private, is visible, it tends to call attention to itself out of all proportion to its economic importance. The result is that the community tends to be awakened to the dangers arising from such activities and such concentration of power before they become so important that it is too late to do anything about them. This phenomenon is very clear for trade unions. Everybody has been reading in the newspapers about the negotiations in steel and has learned that there is a labor problem in the steel industry. The negotiations usually terminate in some kind of wage increase that is regarded as attributable to the union's activities. In the postwar period, domestic servants have gotten larger wage increases without anyone engaging in large-scale negotiations without anyone's knowing that negotiations were going on and without a single newspaper headline, except perhaps to record complaints about the problem of finding domestic servants. I think that trade unions have much monopoly power. But I think that the importance of trade unions is widely exaggerated, that they are nothing like as important in the allocation of labor or the determination of wage rates as they are supposed to be. They are not unimportant—perhaps 10 or 15 percent of the working force have wages now some 10 or 15 percent higher than they otherwise would be because of trade unions; the remaining 85 percent of the working class have wages something like 4 percent lower than they would otherwise be. This is appreciable and important, but it does not give unions the kind of power over the economy that would make it impossible to check their further rise.

The three major sources of strength I have suggested so far are the corroding effect of the extension of state activities and state intervention on attitudes toward the enforcement of the law and on the character of the civil service; the ingenuity of individuals in avoiding regulation; and the visibility of government action and of monopoly. Implicit in these is a fourth, namely, the general inefficiency in the operation of government.

These comments have been rather discursive. I have been attempting simply to list some of the forces at work tending to destroy a free society once established and tending to resist its destruction. I have left out of consideration the force that in some ways is our most important concern, namely, the force of ideas, of people's attitudes about values and about the kind of social organization that they want. I have omitted this force because I have nothing to say about it that is not self-evident.

No very clear conclusion can be drawn from this examination of the forces adverse and favorable to a free society. The historical record suggests pessimism, but the analysis gives no strong basis for either great optimism or confirmed pessimism about the stability of a free society if it is given an opportunity to exist. One of the most important tasks for liberal scholars to undertake is to examine this issue more fully in the light of historical evidence in order that we may have a much better idea of what factors tend to promote and what factors to destroy a free society.

FIVE

AN INTERVIEW WITH MILTON FRIEDMAN:
A *Reason* Interview

(1974)

In February 1974, Senior Editor Tibor Machan, Joe Cobb, and Ralph Raico visited Professor Milton Friedman at his apartment in Chicago and conducted the interview that appears here, after being prepared for publication by Ms. Marty Zupan.

Friedman proved to be an extremely interested, willing, and intensely involved subject of our interview. Through two and one-half hours of uninterrupted exchange, often turning into debate, Friedman covered issues ranging far over the intellectual continuum. The questions, as readers will detect, were not designed to focus exclusively on his own field. Since his economic theories and contributions in general enjoy coverage in both the scholarly and the general media, we attempted to deal with these only as part of a broader exploration of Friedman's perspective.

For all of us this interview turned out to be a challenging experience. We did not shy away from occasional disputes—Friedman himself welcomed the controversies that emerged. Undoubtedly, some people's questions were left unasked. Nevertheless, the final result is presented to our readers with pleasure.

REASON: We'll start out with a ground-level theoretical issue: What is your case for the political system that you advocate? Where do you start from, basically?

FRIEDMAN: I start, I guess, from a belief in individual freedom that derives fundamentally from a belief in the limitations of our knowledge—from a belief in the idea that nobody can be sure that what he believes is right, is *really* right.

REASON: Could you explain why that is your starting point?

FRIEDMAN: I think that the crucial question that anybody who believes in freedom has to ask himself is whether to let another man be free to sin. If you really know what sin is, if you could be absolutely certain that you had the revealed truth, then you could not let another man sin. You *have* to stop him. Of course people will respond that the only virtue in not sinning is if a man chooses of his own free will to avoid it. That argument has a great deal of appeal, but I don't think it's as persuasive as the argument deriving essentially from ignorance. It seems to me unanswerable that if I'm absolutely certain that another man is about to sin, then I am sinning by not preventing him? Under those circumstances, how can you allow a man the freedom to sin? The only answer I can give is that I cannot be absolutely certain that I know what is sin. When I say let another man be free to sin obviously there is appended to that the qualification, provided that in his sinning he is not interfering with the freedom of still other people to do likewise. And that's about where I'd stop on this fundamental philosophical level.

REASON: Well, I will try to pursue this a bit further because, in the context of those who are interested in promoting liberty today, you are in a leadership position, and for that reason a little more scrutiny seems warranted. There is a paradox here at a certain level. You have said that there is at least one thing that you find reasonably certain, that under no circumstances should we interfere with another. But if you admit ignorance in general, then you must yield whenever someone is more certain of a contrary belief.

FRIEDMAN: Subjective certainty is hardly evidence of truth. What you're really saying is you can't get something for nothing. If you're going to have a position, you have to stand *somewhere.* Nihilism would condemn you to suicide—I see no other way to handle a completely nihilistic position. So the question everyone must ask himself is, here I am; I'm an imperfect human being who cannot be certain of anything, so what position can I take? Which involves the least intolerance on my part, the least arrogance, the least expression of belief in my own superior wisdom or knowledge? And it's in this sense that I say that the most attractive position, or the least unattractive position—those are identical—is putting individual freedom first. Because that involves placing least weight on personal views about what's right or wrong. It says that every other man has just as much right to his opinions as I have, provided he doesn't try to interfere with my having my opinion, and that I don't interfere with him.

REASON: But that's where the paradox arises. Mill himself has an example of somebody stepping on a bridge about to collapse, and he asks, am I not caught in a dilemma of either forcing him to save himself if I interfere or of letting a perfectly innocent person be destroyed? Thus sincere people such as Nader push for more regulation. They say, okay, even in the face of dire abuses, are we not then justified to make these moves? And there are clearly some emergency cases when we are, and, if those are admitted, why aren't massive emergency moves admitted? Don't you think, then, that from a point of view of ignorance we may not be as able to defend the value of liberty as from the point of view of a positive thesis that it contributes to good?

FRIEDMAN: In the first place, no principle whatever is really going to give one an unambiguous guide to acts in individual circumstances because every one is a complicated situation, and it's naive to suppose that you can derive from fundamental principles complete rules of conduct. What can be derived from principles are criteria by which to judge conduct but not decisions about conduct. This is one of the places where I have a good deal of criticism of many who call themselves libertarians, who believe that from that single principle they can decide all practical circumstances without knowledge of the particular issues. The second point is that relations between people and individual behavior present separate problems. The belief in freedom provides no guide whatsoever to individual conduct. Robinson Crusoe on an island, with nobody else around, is perfectly free but that doesn't say what action on his part would be regarded as good by him or you or anybody else. Now the positive case for freedom as opposed to the negative case has to do with individual behavior and with the argument that in a free society each individual will have to formulate, and act in accordance with, his own personal values and beliefs and ethics. That's the positive case for freedom.

REASON: Would you consider a hypothetical case that might illuminate something about your basic values? Most economists have been associated with what would generally be considered a utilitarian position. . . .

FRIEDMAN: I myself have never accepted utilitarianism.

REASON: All right. But suppose that the Soviet economy was as productive as capitalism and vice versa but that the capitalist society maintained the individual freedom that you value. Would it be a problem for you to select between those two societies?

FRIEDMAN: It would not be a problem for me to *select*, only to predict. I would *predict* that under those circumstances capitalism would not survive, which doesn't mean that I wouldn't personally prefer it.

REASON: Would you prefer individual freedom even if it meant forgoing a higher material standard of living?

FRIEDMAN: Of course, but there's no dilemma because the only circumstance under which a communist society would have a higher material level of living than a capitalist society—in my opinion—would be one in which the participants preferred other things to a higher material standard of living. But I would go on to predict that a capitalist society under those circumstances could not possibly survive because there are a lot of people who are in favor of free enterprise and a capitalist system only because it delivers the goods. It's fortunate that the capitalist society *is* more productive because if it were not it would never be tolerated. The bias against it is so great that, as it is, it's got to have a five-to-one advantage in order to survive.

REASON: *And* it's touch and go at every moment.

FRIEDMAN: It's touch and go. In fact, I have long believed that there's a strong argument to be made that a free society is a fundamentally unstable equilibrium, in the language of the natural sciences. From a purely scientific point of view, and now I'm going away from philosophy, there's a great deal of basis for believing that a free society is fundamentally unstable—we may regret this but we've got to face up to the facts.

REASON: Do you mean that it's a dynamic system?

FRIEDMAN: No. A stable system can be dynamic—all "dynamic" means is that you have a system in which the variables you are interested in do not have constant state values but are changing all the time. No, I mean something that is much more elementary and simple. I'm not trying to make a very sophisticated point. How often and for how long have we had free societies? For short periods of time. There was an essentially free society in fifth-century Greece. Was it able to survive? It disappeared. Every other time when there's been a free society, it has tended to disappear.

REASON: Perhaps that's an accident.

FRIEDMAN: But if you stop and think, there are certain features about society that give you reason to worry. An authoritarian society has a kind of stability that derives from its monopoly of power and authority. Let me illustrate this in one simple way. We observe and are always asking ourselves the question, why it is that in the Western world intellectuals tend to be collectivists? Certainly one reason is that by nature their whole interest is in questioning things, including whatever society they're in. But in a collectivist society they can't speak up because of suppression, whereas in a free society they can. So the only intellectuals heard from tend to be collectivists. This is an illustration of the kind of forces that make a free society an unstable equilibrium. That doesn't mean we oughtn't try to achieve a free society, to ask ourselves how we can introduce a greater degree of stability. But I think it's the utmost of naivete to suppose that a free society is somehow the natural order of things.

REASON: What about the current situation? How would you assess things today in broad terms and perhaps with some specific recommendations?

FRIEDMAN: Things have been working against us, of course. The direction has been away from freedom and not toward it. There isn't any doubt about the fact. Look at the role of government in the United States, for example. Today government spending at all levels, state, federal, and local, amounts to 40 percent of the total national income. And that's an underestimate of the extent of control that government has over our daily lives. There has been an accumulation of restrictions on individual and human freedom in the past thirty or forty years. Consider the situation right now in Great Britain. Great Britain in the nineteenth century was an essentially free society. It certainly had moved a great deal in the direction of a free society. It's now moving in exactly the opposite direction. It's not at all clear whether Great Britain will be able to remain a free society. If you look over the world as a whole, the dominant feature has been the decline, not the growth, of freedom. I may say that the most discouraging is West Germany. Since the end of World War II Germany has had a tremendous success in every direction by pursuing essentially free enterprise lines. It has done extremely well economically and also in terms of individual freedom. Moreover, there's no other country that has had more experience, of its own and from its neighbors, of collectivists. Yet what do we find? The intellectual community in West Germany has become predominantly collectivist. In West Berlin we see the so-called Free University, facing into the wall that was set up in protest against the West, largely taken over by collectivist groups. Now I find that a very discouraging situation.

REASON: Perhaps we can go back to your comment about intellectuals. What do you think of the theses put forth by von Mises and Schoeck that *envy* motivates many contemporary intellectuals' opposition to the free market?

FRIEDMAN: Well, I don't think we'll get very far by interpreting the intellectuals' motivation. Their critical attitudes might be attributed to personal resentment and envy, but I would say that a more fruitful direction, or a more fundamental one, is that intellectuals are people with something to sell. So the question becomes, what is there a better market for? I think a major reason why intellectuals tend to move toward collectivism is that the collectivist answer is a simple one. If there's something wrong, pass a law and do something about it. If there's something wrong, it's because of some no-good bum, some devil, evil and wicked—that's a very simple story to tell. You don't have to be very smart to write it and you don't have to be very smart to accept it. On the other hand, the individualistic or libertarian argument is a sophisticated and subtle one. If there's something wrong with society, if there's a real social evil, maybe you will make better progress by letting people voluntarily try to eliminate the evil. Therefore, I think, there is in advance a tendency for intellectuals to be attracted to sell the collectivist idea.

REASON: It's paradoxical but people might then say that you are attributing to the collectivist intellectual a better feeling for the market.

FRIEDMAN: Of course. But while there's a bigger market for Fords than there is for American Motors products, there *is* a market for the American Motors products. In the same way, there's a bigger market for collectivist ideology than there is for individualist ideology. The thing that really baffles me is that the fraction of intellectuals who are collectivists is, I think, even larger than would be justified by the market.

REASON: Perhaps we could turn a little bit to your conception of science because one of the widely discussed problems recently is the nature of social sciences as such. Now you are well known for your path-breaking article in *Essays in Positive Economics* dealing with the methodological foundations of your field. It is probably an accurate statement to say that you believe, along with many others of course, that social science can evolve without a place for values in its assessment of human affairs and in its predictions and explanations. What would you say to the argument that this is a mistake because the human animal is just that kind of thing that has value?

FRIEDMAN: I think most of these difficulties are semantic rather than real. Obviously one scientific problem in the social sciences has to do with what values human beings have. How do these values affect their behavior? Are there some consistent tendencies for particular values to develop rather than others? Those are all questions in which the investigator is not imposing his own values. Then no doubt the questions that any particular investigator seeks to pursue depend on what he considers important, which depends on his own values. Certainly the values of the investigator will affect what problems he pursues in the physical sciences as well. The fundamental question from a methodological point of view is whether values enter in any different way than they enter into the study of the physical sciences.

REASON: The suggestion has been made that scientific statements about human affairs involve issues that are value laden, that is, the objects one considers are value laden. For instance the concept "President" is tied up with an entire value system. So when one tries to make a political science judgment about the relationship between President and citizen, one is necessarily involved in implicit valuations because of the concepts at issue.

FRIEDMAN: But none of this constitutes any difference whatsoever between the methodology of the social and the physical sciences. All you're saying is what I said earlier, that among the objects of study in the social sciences are values. Consider the following—I want to make a prediction about the effect on the political system, twenty years from now, of an impeachment and successful conviction of Mr. Nixon. In order to make an objective scientific prediction, I will have to examine the set of values that is now embodied in the concept of the presidency, how the impeachment and conviction of Mr. Nixon would alter those values and how that would alter the political structure of the role of the President. Of course I'm dealing with values at every step, yet the fundamental questions are value free—I'm not saying anything about whether a particular change would be good, bad, or indifferent. Once the scientist has generated a hypothesis, wherever it came from, a crucial scientific question concerns the basis for accepting or rejecting it. And in this sense the natural sciences are on all fours with the social sciences. I've always said that those who maintain a difference between the social and natural sciences are wrong, not about the character of social sciences but about the characteristics they attribute to natural sciences.

REASON: In the approach that you take, say with respect to this impeachment issue, even from your own description there seems to be a model of human beings that enters in—a model to the effect that if something happens in his circumstances, something will happen to the entity, to the individual and his groupings. And those seem to be of a certain kind. Where do you get, in your particular science, that model of man?

FRIEDMAN: Where do biologists get the model of the behavior of the monkey? Predominantly out of the cumulative work in the field. In studying human behavior we have one advantage over the scientist studying monkeys—we are members of the same species that we're studying and therefore have an additional source of information, namely, introspection. But that doesn't alter the character of the pursuit or of the finding. Whether our conclusions are accepted or not does not depend on their introspective certainty but on whether in fact they do predict what happens.

REASON: Could you let us know your thoughts about your son's (David Friedman) recent book, *The Machinery of Freedom,* his anarcho-capitalism, and his suggestions for the maintenance of justice in a free human community.

FRIEDMAN: Well, needless to say, I'm a biased commentator on that. I think it's an extremely good book, which doesn't mean that I agree, necessarily, with all his conclusions. But I think David has done something which it's very important for people who believe in anarcho-capitalism to do, which is to face seriously the hard problems. Take the problem of pollution or the problem of preserving law and order or the problem of enforcing contracts or the problem of defense. These are all real problems. They are not to be dismissed by some appeal that somehow or other the market is ingenious and will solve them. It seems to me that the virtue of David's book is that he faces up to those questions and looks

An Interview with Milton Friedman

seriously at the kinds of institutions that might be developed. All the problems of this class, I might say, reduce to having an arrangement under which people do pay for all the costs they impose on others or for all the benefits they receive from others. The market is most effective and most efficient when that's relatively easy to do. It is least effective and least efficient when that's hard to do.

REASON: Do you agree with his anarcho-capitalism?

FRIEDMAN: I personally would like to believe that an anarchic society is feasible. I do not believe that it is. But at the moment there's a very long way to go before we really get to the point where we part company. There are so many activities of government today which cannot be justified on any grounds whatsoever, *cannot* be justified even by *potential* defects in market arrangements. So we can surely all go a long way down his road before we come to any parting of ways.

REASON: Could you indicate more specifically where you think the weakness in his argument is?

FRIEDMAN: Yes. It has to do with the possibility of developing a substitute for government arrangements to protect against physical coercion. I believe that there must be an ultimate police force. While I think his argument is ingenious—maybe I'm wrong, and I'd like to see somebody experiment with it—it doesn't persuade me that you can avoid the necessity, if you have a community, for an effective government to provide an ultimate monopoly of force.

REASON: Do you think there's a general misunderstanding of your position on gold? It's taken as one of the paradigm cases of your divergence from the general libertarian point of view that you do not believe in a gold-backed money system.

FRIEDMAN: What that reflects is simply a confusion between what I call a real gold standard and a pseudo gold standard. My views on this are stated very clearly in an essay reprinted in

79

my collection of papers, *Dollars and Deficits.* I do not believe in a gold-backed system when that means having the kind of fake gold standard that we had in the United States between 1914 and 1971. I do believe that every individual should be free to own, buy, and sell gold. If under those circumstances a private gold standard emerged, fine, although I make a scientific prediction that it's very unlikely. But I think those people who say they believe in a gold standard are fundamentally being very antilibertarian because what they mean by a gold standard is a governmentally fixed price for gold. It's price fixing. It's what I call the pseudo gold standard. Undoubtedly there is a great deal of misunderstanding on my position on this.

REASON: Do you think there's any genuine hope that in the next decade the Federal Reserve System will bring the rate of monetary expansion down to the level that a free society could live with?

FRIEDMAN: A high rate of monetary expansion would not be desirable, but a free society can live with any rate of monetary expansion, provided there isn't an attempt to eliminate its effects by price and wage controls. What a free society cannot live with is an attempt to repress inflation.

REASON: Do you think that a desirable rate of monetary expansion is very likely to be accomplished?

FRIEDMAN: Yes, but not in the very near future. I think we're going to go through recurrent inflation arising out of overreactions to temporary recessions. I think we are heading for rates of inflation, perhaps 15, 20, 25 percent. We're not heading for a runaway inflation as in Germany after World War I—that only happens if the government has no taxing power at all. But I think we will get increasing rates of inflation. Now after a while people get fed up with it, and it's only then that there is some hope for a reasonable rate of monetary growth. Probably at this stage a precondition for a successful tapering off of inflation is the emergence of a much wider range of escalator clause arrangements, not only in wages, but in mortgages, loans, bank accounts, and so on, all over the economy.

REASON: You recently gave a speech here in Chicago in which you said some rather depressing things about our current situation having to do with free speech and the opportunity to speak one's mind on political issues and so on. Will you elaborate on that for us?

FRIEDMAN: Well, many people argue, as Hayek did so effectively in *The Road to Serfdom,* that there will come a time when the extension of the role of the state will threaten personal freedom. I was saying that that's not a future possibility—it's a present reality. Suppose you look at various classes of society and ask who is really free to express his views on a wide range of subjects without fear of paying any substantial penalty. I think the only people who are really effectively free at the moment are a subset of long-tenured professors in leading universities, only a subset. Consider for a moment the University of Chicago, which I would certainly call a leading university that has always protected individual freedom. Let us suppose that you are a professor of medicine and your research is being financed by the National Institute of Health or the National Science Foundation and you personally believe that it's wrong for government to subsidize medical research. Would you really feel free to get up and make that statement in public? Are the costs greater than you can afford to pay?

REASON: Would you extend this analysis further than academia?

FRIEDMAN: Absolutely. As I said in that speech, the case which is even more obvious is the businessman. There's not a leading businessman in this country who really has freedom of speech. He cannot make a statement and be responsible to the people who hire him, namely, his stockholders, without looking over one shoulder at what the Internal Revenue Service is going to do in response to that statement, over another shoulder at what the Federal Trade Commission is going to do, what the antitrust division is going to do or, right now, what the federal energy office is going to do. The restrictions on personal freedom in the strictest sense of freedom of speech, of freedom of political activity, that now bear on people as a result of the growth of government are very real and very far reaching.

REASON: What do you think, in general, of *Reason?*

FRIEDMAN: I think *Reason* has done well in maintaining a fair amount of tolerance for a variety of views. One of the problems for the general category of publication in which *Reason* falls is that they've tended to become too sectarian and as a result they have very little influence outside the range of the true believers. That doesn't mean that you shouldn't have a firm editorial policy, but I think you ought to keep your columns open to views that you may disagree with. The other thing I might say is that some of the most interesting things that I've seen in *Reason* are articles that offer a substitute for existing policies and not merely philosophical or ideological content. For example, the article some years ago on the jitneys was one of the most useful and effective articles you had. We have to keep on pointing out the way in which actual programs work, whether they be governmental or private, and not simply appeal to first principles all the time. I'm not objecting to having theoretical articles. It's a question of mix.

REASON: Yes, the division of labor applies in the intellectual as any other realm. We have tried to bring out practical-solution type of articles—when we can get them. But sometimes we wonder—there's a rather crude expression about going against the wind whether our time couldn't be invested in some other activity with greater profit for both our ideology and our pockets.

FRIEDMAN: No. Part of our general philosophy is that everybody pursues those things that he thinks valuable. I'm always getting letters—for example, I've written *Newsweek* columns against Social Security. and one of the standard responses I get is from people who want to be put in touch with groups that will organize and do something about this. They want to get together with me and organize a group. My standard response is that I believe in a division of labor—regard my role and my most useful function as being to write and argue about this.

REASON: But you sometimes wish that there was an American Civil Liberties Union that was vigorously protecting the constitutional rights of businessmen and capitalists?

FRIEDMAN: No. I certainly do not. I often say that the two chief enemies of the free society or free enterprise are intellectuals on the one hand and businessmen on the other, for opposite reasons. Every intellectual believes in freedom for himself but is opposed to freedom for others. He thinks that the business world is different, that because of a chaos of competition and waste, there ought to be a central planning board that will establish social priorities. But he's horrified at the thought of having a central planning board to establish social priorities for writers and researchers. So the intellectuals favor freedom for themselves and oppose it for everybody else.

The businessmen are just the opposite—every businessman is in favor of freedom for everybody else, but when it comes to himself that's a different question. He's always the special case. He ought to get special privileges from the government, a tariff, this, that, and the other thing. And it's this coalition that's really difficult for us, so I think we ought to be careful of according businessmen too much power or of believing that they are the major source of support for a free society.

I believe the case for free enterprise, for competition, is that it's the only system that will keep the capitalists from having too much power. There's the old saying, "If you want to catch a thief, set a thief to catch him." The virtue of free enterprise capitalism is that it sets one businessman against another and is thus the most effective device for control.

REASON: Do you have sympathies with the argument for the free society that says that it's based on an inherent sort of psychological egotism—that people naturally pursue their own interests and that can be taken advantage of best in a free market situation.

FRIEDMAN: Sure. People do pursue their own interests, and free enterprise is the kind of arrangement that will enable a large number of people, all pursuing their own interest, to do so most effectively. But it doesn't mean that any free enterprise system or any free market system will do so. People forget the fundamental distinction between Adam Smith's version of the invisible hand and what I suppose you could regard as Bastiat's version. The French idea was that there is somehow a harmony in nature, so that by natural forces if people were left free to pursue their own interests they would benefit everybody. Adam Smith's was a much more subtle and sophisticated argument, that it is possible to set up institutions under which people pursuing their own interests will benefit everybody. His invisible hand required the right set of institutions, and I think that's the case. After all, the distinction between a collectivist society and a market or individualist society is not whether people pursue their own interests. If I take Russia, for example, the people in Russia are all pursuing their own interests, but the institutions set up in Russia make what is in each person's own interest different from what it would be in the United States or in Britain. The manager of a factory in the Soviet Union in pursuing his own interests has to count on the possibility that if he does one thing rather than another he'll get shot. That's one of the sanctions that affects his interests. It doesn't mean he's pursuing some other interest. I don't see how you can think of a world in which people are not pursuing their own interests. What kind of world would that be?

REASON: In a way that becomes definitional: everybody necessarily pursues his own interests. The objection is that there are circumstances in which people can choose not to pursue their own but someone else's interests. Now if you want to say that they are just pursuing their own interests, then it becomes an irrefutable thesis about self-interest.

FRIEDMAN: I understand, but it is true that most people, most of the time, in most societies, are pursuing their narrow self-interest as immediately perceived, neither a long-range nor an altruistic self-interest. I've always viewed the argument for a free society from a somewhat different point of view—how to set up a social arrangement under which the minority can be free to pursue a more far-reaching self-interest? The argument has always been made that the trouble with capitalism is that it's materialistic, while collectivism can afford to pay attention to the nonmaterial. But the experience has been the opposite. There are no societies that have emphasized the purely material requisites of well-being as much as the collectivist. A great majority of people is always concerned with material self-interest, but in collectivist societies that great majority dominates the policy and the minority is suppressed. A free society, a market society, permits those in a minority to pursue their own ends; in fact it is in the free societies that there has been a far greater development of the nonmaterial, spiritual, artistic aspects of well-being. But again it is only possible with the right set of institutions; a capitalist society can suppress freedom as well. Look at many of the South American societies.

REASON: You would consider them capitalistic?

FRIEDMAN: Sure. Capitalism is a necessary condition for a free society but it's not sufficient. Nazi Germany was a capitalist but not a free society.

REASON: This seems strange because ordinarily capitalism is understood to mean the use and disposal of capital on a voluntary basis.

FRIEDMAN: But that's competitive capitalism. Capitalism simply means the private ownership of the means of production.

REASON: But in Nazi Germany production was fully regulated by the state.

FRIEDMAN: Of course. But that's not a question of capitalism but of how universal are the rights of private property or the right of competition. From the point of view of capitalism as traditionally defined, the people who own the means of production might not be able to use it in all possible ways, but they could dispose of it, they could sell it, they could get the proceeds. In the United States every corporation is effectively half owned by the government because the government takes roughly half its profits and shares in half its losses. In that sense you could say the US economy is predominantly socialistic. Even the most purely competitively capitalistic society you can think of would have limitations on what people can do with their property. In the ideal world as conceived by libertarians I would not be free to use my property to hit you over the head.

REASON: For purposes of distinguishing capitalism from other systems, wouldn't the relevant distinction be between use and disposal that necessarily or unavoidably involves somebody else and that which doesn't?

FRIEDMAN: Yes. But this is one of the areas where libertarians are most guilty of not facing up to hard problems. There are no natural rules and definitions of property. There is ultimately an essentially arbitrary element to where we draw the line. What one man may regard as an infringement on property rights, another man may not. Let's take the case of the air space above your land. Is there really going to be any other than an arbitrary decision about how many feet above your house a man can fly before he's violating your air space?

REASON: This becomes a very pragmatic issue because it is by allowing this wide use of the term capitalism—because of its historical association, at least in America, with a free society—that indictments of capitalism qua relying on capital become indictments of the free society. Anything that is bad about the society gets to be called capitalist.

FRIEDMAN: Sure. There's no way of avoiding that. The best remedy is to state clearly what you are in favor of. I'm not in favor of capitalism as such—I'm in favor of competitive capitalism. I'm in favor of free enterprise capitalism, and I'm in favor of laissez-faire subject to general rules and so on. You mustn't get sucked into the trap of defending capitalism as such, including those aspects of it that you don't agree with. After all, getting tariffs was primarily an activity of people you would in every sense call capitalists, and they were promoting their private interest by doing so. There's no inconsistency in saying that you're in favor of competitive capitalism and saying, as I did before, that one of the major threats to a free enterprise system is the businessmen.

REASON: Do you think that a negative income tax and a voucher system are viable for purposes of increasing human freedom and opening up the market, given the political facts of life?

FRIEDMAN: If they are not, I do not know what are. The basic political fact of life is that we must start from where we are now. You cannot hope to get to your ideal except by some intermediate route that will take you from where you are now to where you want to go. If I were starting with a clean slate, in my ideal society I've no idea whether I would be in favor of either the voucher or the negative income tax. Well, actually, with respect to the voucher I would not be in favor of it. In this area I have changed my views somewhat because of evidence that has come up. At one time I thought a strong argument could be made for compulsory schooling because of the harm that the failure to school your child does to other people. In principle one cannot reject compulsory schooling as a desirable thing. But the work that Ed West and others have done on the actual development of schools makes it abundantly clear that in the absence of compulsory schooling there would nonetheless be a very high degree of literacy—that self-interest would be sufficient to yield a degree of schooling that would satisfy the social need for a literate society. Consequently, I am no longer in favor of compulsory schooling. If you're not in favor of compulsory schooling, there's no reason to have a voucher system.

REASON: What about starting from where we are now?

FRIEDMAN: The voucher scheme is the only one I've come across that offers some improvement, that introduces a larger degree of market forces and, more important, that offers a possible route to getting rid of governmental financing altogether. Because once the voucher—fixed sum—is introduced and market schools are introduced, which would have to be done under a sensible voucher scheme, then there's a chance that the voucher will wither away, that the size of the voucher will stay the same while, through inflation and real income growth, it will come to constitute a smaller and a smaller part of the total cost of schooling.

REASON: Would you also hold that in a free society there would be no place for the negative income tax?

FRIEDMAN: There I'm not so sure what my attitude would be if we were starting from a clean slate. I do believe that a case can be established for joint action to help people in dire distress. This is one of these problems of external effects where I am benefited if you help somebody who is poor, just as I benefit from your educating your child. It might be that joint action such as the negative income tax is unnecessary; my own belief is that voluntary charity would probably be more than sufficient to eliminate acute distress. But that's a practical conclusion; it's not grounded on principle, in that a free society would not necessarily rule out arrangements under which 90 percent of us agree to impose taxes on ourselves to keep the other 10 percent from dire distress.

The fundamental underlying principle of a free society has to be unanimity—but it is not capable of being achieved. The virtue of a market arrangement is that unanimity is achieved without any measure of coercion, and wherever that's feasible through a market arrangement, fine. But it isn't always. How does one deal with the case where what literal unanimity requires is that I agree to contribute on the assumption that everybody else agrees? The fundamental problem in achieving unanimity is transaction costs. The argument often given is that, if everybody is in favor of it then they can voluntarily come to agreement, but this avoids the hard issue of the cost of making such an arrangement. That's why I say that my concept of a free society does not exclude the use of governmental arrangements in those cases where transaction costs are so high that we are willing to accept, as it were, being overruled in some cases to avoid the transaction costs involved in achieving true unanimity.

REASON: But aren't you opening the floodgates for comprehensive entry of government when you argue that because this is a distress situation we should allow the government to come in? Every time Ralph Nader stands up and makes a case it's something "very distressing and upsetting". . . .

FRIEDMAN: Well, first of all, you're empirically wrong. Consider the American experience. We had a limited government, which, from the Revolution to 1930, did not in fact expand greatly. Except for a period of major war all governments, federal, state, and local, never spent more than 10 percent to 15 percent of the total national income. The floodgates had been opened and there was no flood. Secondly, you can't avoid opening those gates. The empirical experience is that when voluntary arrangements were relied on people objected so much that government got into the act. Isn't it better to recognize that we're going to live in a mixed world than to say, "Oh, my God, we won't do anything through government because once we do any little thing we have a flood."

REASON: The alternative is not anarchism.

FRIEDMAN: But it is.

REASON: No. The proper role of government would be adjudication and crime prevention because there force is involved. But where there's no force involved—the crippled children are unfortunate and not made crippled by criminals—then there is no place for the government because no injustice has been done to those people and there is nothing for the government to adjudicate or prevent.

FRIEDMAN: But your floodgate is opened.

REASON: No, because prevention of coercion is a very limited area of operation that is specifiable and the criterion can be ascertained. The distinction is voluntary/involuntary.

FRIEDMAN: You are kidding yourself, as you would find out if you tried to pin down precisely what actions constitute coercion, what actions are voluntary, and what actions are involuntary. But, in any event, we've gone a long way away from the issue of the negative income tax.

REASON: But it all ties together. A number of people who oppose that program maintain that you are introducing government in an area where no force exists and that the only justifiable role for government is where there is coercion.

FRIEDMAN: If we go back to the negative income tax, the argument you're now making is relevant only to whether, starting from a clean slate, it should be introduced. But it's utterly irrelevant to the present question, which is how to get government out of an area where it's already strongly entrenched.

REASON: One of the objections offered against your suggestion is that to introduce negative income tax measures allows for the development of another bureaucracy that is going to be self-perpetuating and that it's illusory to think that it's going to put itself out of business.

FRIEDMAN: The question is, how do you substitute for the present bureaucracy one that there's at least some chance of reducing in the future? And the fundamental tactic in all of these cases is the same—you cannot move from where you are now to where you want to go by abolishing what you now have. So the method is to get the present bureaucracy to operate a system that has some self-destructive features—give that bureaucracy a different function but a function that there is at least some chance will wither away. I don't see any alternative tactic, and I wonder what alternatives the critics of these schemes can come up with.

REASON: One of the alternatives that they might raise is to tackle the problem from a different direction, something like law, referenda, politicians, and so on. Get some free market congressmen and free market senators. . . .

FRIEDMAN: But what do we want them to vote for? The negative income tax and the voucher scheme are both devices for enabling the free market to play a larger role, and it's not an answer to say we want to get free market congressmen. Do you really think that there's any possibility that a Congress, even one including people who oppose the negative income tax, would vote to eliminate welfare overnight? Entirely aside from the force of the bureaucracy, it would be an utterly inhuman thing to do. We, through government, have induced millions of people to be dependent on welfare who would never have been dependent on it if we hadn't started out on this line thirty or forty years ago. Can we overnight throw them on the streets?

REASON: Some people would probably say yes; their argument is, "It's not my responsibility—I never voted for those things, I never induced anybody to go on welfare. Maybe I will help these people once the laws are off the books, but as long as they are living off these coercive laws I'm going to do everything to eliminate the laws and then take care of the problem when it arises later." That may be heartless in your view, but it's a firmly held position by some.

FRIEDMAN: Well, I understand the position but I think that is not an effective way to achieve their own objectives. I don't think a revolutionary, once-and-for-all approach will succeed. As I said earlier, I think the odds are that a free society is on the way out but that doesn't mean that we shouldn't fight for it or that sulking in our tents explaining to one another how nice it would be if we could only wipe the slate clean and get our way is an effective means of fighting for a free society.

SIX

SAY "NO" TO INTOLERANCE

(1991)

Thank you very much. I'm embarrassed by that introduction and by your welcoming of me because I'm afraid that you might not be quite so enthusiastic at the end of the talk. The virtue of being among people with whom you agree fundamentally is that you can talk about some of the harder issues, which you don't want to talk about in other circles. I want tonight to talk about basic libertarian beliefs and values. (I refer to myself as a liberal in the true meaning of that term: a believer in freedom. Unfortunately, we've had to use the word "libertarian" because, as Schumpeter said, "As a supreme if unintended compliment, the enemies of the system of private enterprise have thought it wise to appropriate its label.") As a longtime liberal-libertarian, I am puzzled by a paradox. On the one hand, I regard the basic human value that underlies my own beliefs as tolerance, based on humility. I have no right to coerce someone else because I cannot be sure that I am right and he is wrong. On the other hand—and this is the paradox—some of our heroes, people who have done the most to promote libertarian ideas, have been highly intolerant as human beings and have justified their views (with which I largely agree) in ways that I regard as promoting intolerance. Equally important, as I have observed the libertarian movement, there's a related strand of utopianism in the libertarian movement that I believe is also productive of intolerance and is fundamentally inconsistent with the basic values that I believe we stand for.

Why do I regard tolerance as the foundation of my belief in freedom? How do we justify not initiating coercion? If I asked you what is the basic philosophy of a libertarian, I believe that most of you would say that a libertarian philosophy is based on the premise that you should not initiate force, that you may not initiate coercion. Why not?

If we see someone doing something wrong, someone starting to sin (to use a theological term), let alone just make a simple mistake, how do we justify not initiating coercion? Are we not sinning if we don't stop him? Only two bases for a negative answer occur to me that make any sense. One—which I regard as largely an evasion—is that there's no virtue in his not sinning if he's not free to sin. That may be true. But then that doesn't apply to me. It may be no virtue for him. That doesn't mean I should let him sin: Am I not sinning when I let him sin? How do I justify letting him sin? I believe that the more persuasive answer is, can I be sure he's sinning? Can I be sure that I am right and he is wrong? That I know what sin is?

This is a complicated and difficult problem. Let me give an extreme example. I am on the Golden Gate Bridge and I see someone getting ready to jump. He's going to commit suicide. Am I entitled to use physical coercion to stop him, assuming that I am capable of doing so? On the libertarian basis of not initiating coercion, one would have to say no. Yet I am sure that most of you, like me, would stop him if we could. We'd grab him. We'd justify that temporarily by saying, "He doesn't really intend to do that and it's irreversible, and we've got to stop him from doing something irreversible."

We grab him. We hold on to him. And he gives a perfectly plausible reason why he wants to commit suicide. Are you going to let him go? In principle you should say yes. In practice, I doubt very much that many of us, assuming that we had the power to hold him, would just let him go.

What this demonstrates, fundamentally, is that no simple principle is really adequate. We do not have all the answers, and there is no simple formula that will give us all the answers. That's why humility, tolerance, is so basic, so fundamental. Because the only way that we can get a little closer to those fundamental principles is by being tolerant, by considering and respecting the opinions of people who disagree with us.

And yet, as I've already said, how can we square that with the intolerance demonstrated by people who deservedly are heroes to libertarians? There is no doubt in my mind that Ludwig von Mises has done more to spread the fundamental ideas of free markets than any other individual. There is no doubt in my mind that nobody has done more than Ayn Rand to develop a popular following for many of these ideas. And yet there is also no doubt that both of them were extremely intolerant.

I recall a personal episode, at the first meeting of the Mont Pelerin Society—the founding meeting in 1947 in Mont Pelerin, Switzerland. Ludwig von Mises was one of the people who was there. I was also. The group had a series of discussions on different topics. One afternoon the discussion was on the distribution of income, taxes, progressive taxes, and so on. The people in that room included Friedrich von Hayek, Fritz Machlup, George Stigler, Frank Knight, Henry Hazlitt, John Jewkes, Lionel Robbins, Leonard Read—hardly a group whom you would regard as leftists. In the middle of that discussion von Mises got up and said, "You're all a bunch of socialists" and stomped out of the room.

You need only read Barbara Branden's *The Passion of Ayn Rand,* a fascinating book, to recognize that what I've said applies to Rand as well. Barbara Branden tells a story that refers to both Rand and von Mises: "One evening, the Hazlitts [that was Henry Hazlitt, whom I mentioned] invited Ayn and Frank to dinner with Dr. and Mrs. von Mises. The evening was a disaster. It was the first time Ayn had discussed moral philosophy in depth with either of the two men. 'My impression,' she was to say, 'was that von Mises did not care to consider moral issues, and Henry was seriously committed to altruism. . . . We argued quite violently. At one point von Mises lost his patience and screamed at me. We did not part enemies—except for von Mises at the moment; about a year later he and I met at a conservative dinner and his wife made peace between us.'"

The important thing to me is less their intolerance in personal behavior than the philosophical doctrines on which they claimed to base their views, which seem to me to be fundamentally a source of intellectual intolerance. So far as von Mises is concerned, I refer to his methodological doctrine of praxeology. That's a fancy word and may seem highly irrelevant to my topic, but it isn't at all. Because his fundamental idea was that we knew things about "human action" (the title of his famous book) because we are human beings. As a result, he argued, we have absolutely certain knowledge of the motivations of human action and, he maintained, that we can derive substantive conclusions from that basic knowledge. Facts, statistical, or other evidence cannot, he argued, be used to test those conclusions but only to illustrate a theory. They cannot be used to contradict a theory because we are not generalizing from observed evidence but from innate knowledge of human motives and behavior.

That philosophy converts an asserted body of substantive conclusions into a religion. They do not constitute a set of scientific propositions that you can argue about in terms of empirical evidence. Suppose two people who share von Mises's praxeological view come to contradictory conclusions about anything. How can they reconcile their difference? The only way they can do so is by a purely logical argument. One has to say to the other,

"You made a mistake in reasoning." And the other has to say, "No, you made a mistake in reasoning." Suppose neither believes he has made a mistake in reasoning. There's only one thing left to do: fight. Karl Popper—another Austrian, like Mises and Hayek—takes a different approach. If we disagree we can say to one another, "You tell me what facts, if they were observed, you would regard as sufficient to contradict your view." And vice versa. Then we can go out and see which, if either, conclusion the evidence contradicts. The virtue of this modern scientific approach, as proposed by Popper, is that it provides a way in which, at least in principle, we can resolve disagreements without a conflict.

So much for von Mises. That's a very brief statement, and I recognize that it doesn't do justice to either praxeology or Popper. But that's not relevant here.

The same thing is true of Ayn Rand, as her phrase about Hazlitt's supposed commitment to altruism suggests. Rand did not regard facts as relevant, as ways of testing her propositions. She derived everything from the basic proposition that A is A. And from that follows everything. But if it does, again suppose two Objectivists, two disciples of Ayn Rand, disagree or that a disciple disagrees with her. Both agree that A is A. There's no disagreement about that. But for one reason or another they have different views on another subject. How do they reconcile that difference? There is no way. And that's the basic reason for the stories that Barbara Branden tells in *The Passion of Ayn Rand* about what happened when people disagreed in any minute detail with Ayn Rand.

I believe that there's an enormous paradox there. But don't misunderstand me. Nothing I say lessens my admiration in any way for the role that both von Mises and Rand played in promoting the ideas of liberty and free markets. And yet I believe that they teach both a positive and a negative lesson. The negative lesson is that we must beware of intolerance if we're going to be really effective in persuading people. The writings of both Rand and Mises—and much libertarian literature—take for granted that hard questions have easy answers, that it's possible to know something about the real world, to derive substantive conclusions, from purely a priori principles.

Let me take a real example. How many times have you heard someone say that the answer to a problem is that you simply have to make it private property. But is private property such an obvious notion? Does it come out of the soul?

I have a house. It belongs to me. You fly an airplane over my house, 20,000 feet up. Are you violating my private property? You fly over at 50 feet. You might give a different answer. Your house is next door. You have a hi-fi system. You play your hi-fi at an enormously high decibel count. Are you violating my private property? Those are questions to which you can't get answers by introspection or asking whether A is A or not. They are practical questions that require answers based on experience. Before there were airplanes, nobody thought of the problem of trespass through air. So simply saying private property is a mantra, not an answer. Simply saying use the market is not an answer.

Let me give you two recent examples that also are relevant to the same theme—utopianism. I'll touch on them very briefly: vouchers and negative income tax. Re vouchers—and I'm now speaking of schooling vouchers—schooling is, next only to national defense, the largest socialist enterprise in the United States. And it is clearly as much of a failure as the socialist enterprises in Poland or Hungary or Czechoslovakia or East Germany. It shares the characteristic features of those failures. The characteristic feature of socialist failure is that you have a group, the *nomenklatura,* who do very well, you have masses who do very poorly, and the system as a whole is highly inefficient. That's exactly the case with our school system. Those of us who happen to live in high-income suburbs, as well as high-paid teachers and teacher-administrators, do very well out of the system. The poor suckers who live in the ghetto or who don't have any money, they do very poorly out of the system. The system as a whole takes two or three times as many resources to operate as are necessary, and it doesn't do a good job when it does. So it's clearly a failure.

In the Future of Freedom Foundation's *Freedom Daily,* for September 1990—again, a group that is doing good work and is making an impact—Jacob Hornberger wrote, "What is the answer to socialism in public schools? Freedom." Correct. But how do we get from here to there? Is that somebody else's problem? Is that a purely practical problem that we can dismiss? The ultimate goal we would like to get to is a society in which people are responsible for themselves and for their children's schooling. And in which you do not have a governmental system. But am I a statist, as I have been labeled by a number of libertarians, because some thirty years ago I suggested the use of educational vouchers as a way of easing the transition? Is that, and I quote Hornberger again, "simply a futile attempt to make socialism work more efficiently"? I don't believe it. I don't believe that you can simply say what the ideal is. This is what I mean by the utopian strand in libertarianism. You cannot simply describe the utopian solution and leave it to somebody else how we get from here to there. That's not only a practical problem. It's a problem of the responsibilities that we have.

The same issue arises with respect to welfare, Social Security, and the rest. It may be that the ideal is—and I believe that it is— to have a society in which you do not have any kind of major or substantial governmental system of welfare. Again, nearly thirty years ago I suggested, as a way of promoting a transition from here to there, a negative income tax as a substitute for and alternative to the present ragbag of welfare and redistributionist measures. Again, is that a statist solution? I believe not. We have participated in a society in which people have become dependent on government handouts. It is irresponsible, immoral I would say, simply to say, "Oh well, somehow or other we'll overnight drop the whole thing." You have to have some mechanism of going from here to there. I believe that we lose a lot of plausibility for our ideas by not facing up to that responsibility.

It is of course desirable to have a vision of the ideal, of Utopia. Far be it from me to denigrate that. But we can't stop there. If we do, we become a cult or a religion, not a living, vital force. These comments apply, I believe, to the largest socialist enterprise in the United States, that is, of course, national defense. Like everyone else in this room, I am appalled by the waste of the defense industry. I am sure that if you and I could only run it, we could do it for half the money and do it a lot better. But although I have tried for many years to figure out a way in which we could run defense as a private enterprise and despite the hopes of some anarchist libertarians like my son, that we can, I have to admit that after some thirty years now, he's never been able to persuade me that we could. I suppose that just shows how intolerant I am. At any rate, simple slogans like "The market will take care of it" or "noninterventionism" do not resolve the hard problems. We may very well agree on the direction we want to go in, but just how we're going to go there and how far we're going to go, that's a much more difficult problem.

Let me close by noting that admirers of von Mises seldom quote the following of his statements: "Government as such is not only not an evil but the most necessary and beneficial institution, as without it no lasting cooperation and no civilization could be developed and preserved." Now that's an idea to chew over. Thank you very much.

SEVEN

THE LINE WE DARE NOT CROSS

(1976)

Those of us who have been fortunate enough to be born in the United States in the twentieth century naturally take freedom for granted: it seems to us that a relatively free society is the natural state of mankind. But that is a great misconception. Freedom is very far from being the natural state of mankind; on the contrary, it is an extraordinarily unusual situation. If one looks back through history, in any place on the globe, one finds that the natural state of mankind in most periods in history has been tyranny and misery. If one looks over the globe geographically at any point in time, one finds that most of the people in the world were living in a state of tyranny and misery.

The periods and places in which there has been something approaching a free society have been few and far between. There was a small example in the 5th century, B.C., on the Peloponnesian peninsula, in Athens; but that was only a partly free society. It was a society that was free for the citizens of Athens, but not for the slaves who also inhabited the city. There is a brief spurt of freedom during the Renaissance in the Middle Ages. The most extended period of freedom has been the period in the eighteenth, nineteenth, and early twentieth centuries in Western Europe and the United States. Yet look at how fragile that freedom has been.

The countries in the world that have been able to maintain during that period something roughly approaching a free society are few in number. They consist almost entirely of the English-speaking and Scandinavian countries.

This fragility of freedom was brought home to me dramatically last year when I spent a week in a small South American country. I was in Chile as part of a group that was examining and considering the economic problems which Chile was then facing—problems that we are likely to have in our future (I hope in a very distant future). They were problems that were epitomized by the fact that they had managed after great effort to bring the rate of inflation down from 900 percent a year to 400 percent a year.

Chile, of course, is very different; it is, for one thing, a very much poorer country than the United States. Yet the history of Chile is highly relevant to our present situation and our future problems. Of all the South American countries, Chile had about the longest history of a reasonable degree of democratic government and a reasonably free society, a history which dates back to the nineteenth century.

The present problems in Chile, which has lost its freedom and which today is governed by an authoritarian regime, had their origin in my opinion, some fifty or sixty years ago. Chile was not only one of the countries in South America that had the longest history of liberty and political democracy, but it was also one of the earliest countries in South America to institute a welfare state and welfare state measures. I was surprised to find in reading about Chile that, like Great Britain, the class of measures that we today associate with welfare statism, the New Deal, and the Fair Deal got their start in Chile about 1906, 1907, or 1908, at about the same time that they started in Westminster.

The present state of Chile, in my opinion, is the end result of an expansion in the role of government over the lives of people. The important thing about that development—and the main lesson I am going to try to elaborate in this article—is that the measures that led to that result were introduced by good people for good objectives. The measures that led to Chile's crisis were not bad measures that were taken by bad people with the aim of grinding the poor under their heels. On the contrary, the problems of Chile derived from the attempt to use the state and the political mechanism to achieve high-minded objectives. That development led to an increasing expansion in the role of the state in the society, and it led to an increasing accumulation of legislation in which the government controlled what people could and could not do. The obvious numerical counterpart of this was an increase in government spending until, by the time Salvadore Allende came to power in Chile, government spending had reached something like 40 percent of the national income.

Since Chile was a poor country, it was difficult to impose explicit taxes to generate revenues of 40 percent of national income. As a result, taxes were imposed indirectly in the form of inflation. There is a great misconception about what happened. Allende, who produced the great confrontation and was clearly seeking to turn Chile into a communist state, was only carrying out the laws that had already been enacted by his predecessors. He introduced very little that was radically different. He just continued in the same direction that policy had been proceeding, ever more rapidly, during the past thirty to forty years. However, the end result was the tipping point at which the willingness of the public to put up with increasing involvement in their lives was exceeded. There was first, the Allende régime with its threat of a left-wing dictatorship, and then a counterrevolution with the military taking over and a military junta being established, which also is very far indeed from a free society. It, too, is an authoritarian society that denies the liberties and freedoms of the people in the sense in which Anglo-Saxon democrats conceive of them.

Lest you think that this tale of the history of Chile need not concern us, let me ask you to consider a case much closer. Cast your eyes across the Atlantic to the home of most of the ideas of freedom that we cherish—to the United Kingdom (UK). Britain is a much richer country than Chile. It has a far stronger tradition of a belief in freedom and in democratic rights. Yet the UK is going down the same path as Chile and, I fear, is headed for the same end. It is almost impossible for any one of us brought up in the great traditions emanating from Great Britain—the noble tradition of freedom and of democratic rights starting with the Magna Carta and coming down through the whole list of famous Englishmen who have written and taught us about free institutions—it is almost impossible for anyone brought up in that tradition to utter the words that Britain is in danger of losing freedom and democracy; and yet it is a fact! I was lecturing in England a year or so ago, and it was precisely because I had spent some time in the British Isles and had seen what was happening there that I was so much reminded in Chile this spring that I was seeing the same scene over again. It was like a continuous movie, and this was where I came in. Or maybe I should say this was where I went out.

About the same time as Chile, Great Britain started on the welfare state line. In 1913, a great English constitutional lawyer, A. V. Dicey, added a new preface to a second edition of a series of lectures he had given in America at the turn of the century under the title *Relation between Law and Public Opinion in the Nineteenth Century.* In this preface, referring to the measures that Britain had already taken by 1913, particularly in the area of old-age benefits and of the treatment of people in institutions, he said,

> This is a road on which no reasonable man can refuse to enter, but once entered nobody can tell where it is going to lead.

That was an extraordinarily prescient prediction of what was in store for Britain because the role of the government has, from that point to this, expanded until today (again by that simple numerical measure that I used) total government spending in

Great Britain (central and local) amounts to some 60 percent of the national income.

And yet there is enormous pressure for still more government spending. Nobody is satisfied; everybody is dissatisfied. Society is being polarized. It is hard to see how Britain can avoid the fate that Chile experienced. Lest I seem singularly alarmist, I can also cite Eric Sevareid, who in one of his broadcast commentaries over the network after a visit to Britain, made exactly this analogy ("Britain is on the verge of the Allende period of Chile"). I fear very much that the odds are at least 50–50 that within the next five years British freedom and democracy, as we have seen it, will be destroyed.

But, again, I need not go that far away. Let me come closer to home. Consider at the moment New York City.

New York City displays precisely the same trends as Chile and the United Kingdom. New York City has the dubious distinction of having the most welfare-state-oriented electorate in the country. It has been following the same policy of ever-growing governmental involvement in the affairs of its citizens, and the result has been exactly the same. Wherever this path has been followed, whether in Chile or in the UK or in New York, it has two consequences. The first is financial crisis. That clearly characterized the situation in Chile. That clearly characterizes the situation in the UK where the rate of inflation reached something over 25 percent; where the government budget is enormously in deficit; where Britain is able to survive primarily by borrowing from overseas. Similarly in New York, the first effect—financial crisis—is obvious.

The second effect is less obvious. This path leads not only to financial crisis but also to a loss of liberty and freedom, and New York City has lost its liberty and freedom. New York City is no longer being governed by the citizens of New York City or by people elected by the citizens of New York City. It is now being governed by a committee of overseers appointed by the State of New York with power to overrule the elected officials of the City of New York. This loss of self-government and freedom has been concealed by the shift of power from one democratic institution, the City of New York, to another democratic institution, the State of New York. But the principle is the same: financial crisis leads to a loss of self-government. There is only one important difference between New York City, on the one hand, and Chile or the United Kingdom on the other, and that is that New York City does not have one of those printing presses on which you can turn out green pieces of paper that people call money. It cannot issue its own money. Chile and Britain could issue their own money, and therefore the financial crisis took the form of inflation, whereas in New York it degenerated more promptly to bankruptcy.

Let me come still closer to home. For the period from the founding of this country to 1929, leaving aside periods of major wars such as the Civil War and the First World War and the Revolution, total government spending in the United States (federal, state, and local) never exceeded 10 percent of the income of the people. State and local expenditure (more immediately subject to the control of the citizenry) was twice as large during that period as federal government expenditure. Total federal government expenditure in 1929 was 3 percent of the national income. In the forty-five years since, total governmental expenditures have risen to 40 percent of the national income in the United States, and federal government spending is twice as much as state and local spending. Federal spending today is something like 25 percent of the national income, or roughly ten times as large as it was in 1929.

I submit that we have been moving in the same direction as Chile and Britain and New York and that we have been experiencing signs of financial crisis: the emergence of inflation at a higher and higher rate. We have also been experiencing the second effect: the loss of freedom.

People always talk as if the problem is in the future, as if the problem is that individual freedom is threatened by the encroaching control of our lives by the state. It is not merely the future, however, it is the present; for freedom has already been greatly reduced in many dimensions. After all, the spending of 40 percent of our income for us by government is a restriction on our freedom. We have nothing to say about that 40 percent except through the political process (to which I will come in a moment). But put aside the question of income. Go to those more fundamental freedoms of speech, of belief, of personal behavior, for they, too, have been severely restricted. Consider for a moment the simple question of freedom of speech. Let me ask this: How often does one read in the papers any statement on public issues by a major businessman or industrialist except where it immediately concerns his own enterprise?

A little over a year ago, President Ford constructed a program, hastily buried shortly thereafter, the WIN Program (for Whip Inflation Now). Now it was a program that had some good things and some bad things, but taken as a whole it was a pretty silly program. Yet one can search every newspaper in the United States without finding a single major businessman who made a public statement against that program. Why? Was it because they agreed with it? It is inconceivable; at least it is inconceivable that they unanimously agreed with it. Surely there was some businessman who didn't.

However, a businessman at the head of a great corporation thinks three times before he speaks out on a major public issue. He looks over his left shoulder and sees the Internal Revenue Service getting ready to come and audit his accounts, and he looks over his right shoulder and sees the Department of Justice standing only too ready to launch an antitrust suit against him. And then, if he has more shoulders than two, he asks what the Federal Trade Commission is going to do about his advertising;

and what the Food and Drug Administration is going to do about the products he produces; and what is the Safety Council going to do about this, that, and the other thing? You are not free to speak if you are in that position.

Let me get even closer to home. Let me get to my own area: the academy. Is the scholar free to speak? I ask myself whether the professors who teach medicine at any American medical school in this country, most of whose research is being financed by the National Institutes of Health, whether they really feel free to speak out against socialized medicine and against further involvement of the government in medicine. Some of them obviously will. But is there the slightest doubt, to use those famous words of the Supreme Court, that their dependence for the major source of their financing on the federal government has a "chilling effect" on the freedom of speech? About the only people who now have full freedom of speech are people in the fortunate position that I am in: a tenured professor at a major private academic institution on the verge of retirement.

The Department of Health, Education, and Welfare in Washington seeks to impose on educational institution requirements that, in my opinion, would interfere severely and seriously with scholarly performance. Every academic institution in the United States is threatened in exactly the same way. If it were not so serious, it would be humorous because there is no group in this country that has done more to bring this upon themselves than the academic community. We have been in the forefront in persuading the public at large that the doctrine of individual responsibility is a false doctrine; that the source of all good things is Big Brother in Washington. We only complain when it comes home and hits us.

Let me move from description to analysis. What is the explanation? Why does the attempt to use the political market to achieve noble objectives go awry and destroy our freedom? Why does it happen? In the simplest form, the fundamental fallacy of the welfare state that leads to both financial crisis and the destruction of freedom is the attempt to do good at somebody else's expense. That is the fundament fallacy. First, nobody spends somebody else's money as carefully as he spends his own. That is why trying to do good at someone else's expense leads to financial crisis.

Second, if you are going to do good at somebody else's expense, you have to take the money away from him. So force, coercion, destruction of freedom is at the very bottom, at the very source, of the attempts to do good at somebody else's expense. Some years ago, in an article published in the *New York Times Magazine,* John Kenneth Galbraith said that there was no problem in New York City that would not be solved if the city government's budget was doubled. In the interim the city government's budget has been quadrupled and so have the problems. And the reason is straightforward. While the city government had *more* to spend, the citizens had *less* to spend because the government can only get the money by taking it away from somebody else.

More fundamentally, what is at the base of our problem is the failure to recognize the distinction between the political market, on the one hand, and the economic market, on the other. This distinction, which I would like to develop, is one that can be expressed in various terms—my professional background leads me to put it in economic terms. The political system is a marketplace; the economic system is a marketplace. These are two different kinds of market mechanisms, and they have very different consequences. Though it may seem a paradox, the economic market is a freer, more democratic market than the political marketplace.

Let me at the outset put to one side a false distinction between the two markets. We tend to be misled by words. Because we speak of a person in the economic market as having a private enterprise, we think of him as serving his *private* interest. Because we speak of a government bureaucrat as being a public servant, we speak of him as serving the *public* interest. But that is an utterly false distinction. Almost every individual serves his own private interest: that interest need not be pecuniary; it need not be narrowly physical or material. The great saints of history have served their private interest just as the most money-grubbing miser has served his private interest. The *private interest* is whatever it is that drives an individual. A government bureaucrat is seeking to serve his private interest just as much as you or I or the ordinary businessman. To make this point in an extreme form, compare the manager of a Russian factory who is a public servant and the manager of an American factory who is supposedly a private employee. They both are serving their self-interest; the only difference is that the actions that will serve their self-interest are different. The American manager has to worry about getting fired; the Soviet manager has to worry about getting fired at! And that makes a big difference in what is actually in each man's self-interest.

In exactly the same way, the bureaucrats at Health, Education, and Welfare in Washington who are trying to extend their control and impose regulations on universities and colleges throughout the land are serving their private interest. They may believe thoroughly in what they are doing, but they are nonetheless serving their private interest in seeking to extend the scope of their power, importance, and influence. It is a myth that there is a difference between the motives of the people who are employed in government and the people who are employed in the private sector. That is equally true of those who are competing for votes; for the legislators are competing one with another, competing for votes, and it is in their private interest to do those things that will get them enough votes to get elected.

A second myth about the political market is that, as opposed to the economic market in which individuals vote with dollars, in the political market there is one-person/one-vote. That is true on a formal level, but it is obviously false on a realistic level. It is a system in which there is highly weighted voting, in which some people have an enormously greater influence on the political outcome than others. This is obvious in all sorts of ways; one need only take the most dramatic example at the moment. We have a great dispute in this country about "forced busing." Whatever may be said for or against it, there is not the slightest doubt that 80–90 percent of both whites and blacks in this country are opposed to forced busing. Yet we have it, and we are going to continue to have it. How can one explain that on the basis of one-person/one-vote?

There is a highly weighted voting system, and an analysis of the political market must investigate why it exists. Is the problem with the political market that there are "wicked people"? No, the individuals who operate in the political market are just as wicked or just as noble as the individuals who operate in the economic market. They are the same people. The difference is the structure of the market. It is that the political market is a system under which all decisions have to be *yes* or *no.*

The fundamental difference between the political market and the economic market is that in the political market there is very little relation between what you vote for and what you get. In the economic market you get what you vote for. Let me give you a very trivial example of the kind of thing that I have in mind.

Let us suppose the question at issue is whether neckties should be red or green. If that is going to be decided by a political mechanism, everybody votes. If 51 percent of the people vote that ties shall be red, 100 percent of the people get red neckties. In the economic market each one of us goes to the shopping center separately. If 51 percent of the people vote that ties shall be red, 51 percent get red neckties and 49 percent get green neckties. Everybody gets what he votes for—and this is a fundamental difference between the two markets.

There are some things for which the vote has to be *yes* or *no:* things that are the appropriate function and role of government. There is no way in which 51 percent of the people in the United States can be at war in Vietnam and 49 percent of the people can be not at war—that is precisely the kind of a decision that has to be decided through a mechanism which permits a *yes/no* vote. The problem is that we have extended the political market beyond things of that kind and to the kind of things where it is possible for each person to get what he votes for, where we do not have to have a *yes* or *no* decision. If you have a *yes* or *no* decision, then there is almost always a very loose or no relation between your vote and the result. As a consequence, you do not in general have any incentive to examine thoroughly the issue you vote on, that is, to vote intelligently. In the political market this phenomenon leads to weighted voting in favor of *special* interests and opposed to the *general* interest. If I have some piece of legislation that is going to benefit a small group a great deal, the members of that small group have a real incentive to learn about the issue, to bring pressure on their legislators to lobby for it in Washington. The rest of us? Here is something which is going to mean millions of dollars separately to each of a small number of people, but to you and me it means fifty cents extra on our tax bill. What incentive do we have to find out about it or to spend any time voting intelligently? or to bring pressure on our legislators?

A few very simple examples. About three or four years ago the then President Nixon tried to eliminate a program under which the federal government had for many years been subsidizing people who tasted tea. This is literally true. This is a program under which the government graded tea for the benefit of importers, and we paid taxes to hire people to taste the tea and decide what grade it should get. It is very hard to see any general public interest in that—after all, the tea industry can provide those people. Nixon made the simple, obvious proposal that we should eliminate it. We still have that program because the people in the tea industry were up in arms about it; they didn't want to have that little item taken away from them. Is there anybody in the vast American electorate who would take his vote away from a representative because that representative voted to keep the tea-tasting arrangement?

Let me offer a more important case. We have a US postal system that I would hardly suppose is distinguished for its efficiency. For many years I have been urging the elimination of the monopoly privileges of the Post Office: opening it up to competition. About a dozen years ago, I talked to a good friend of mine who was then in Congress to urge him to introduce a one-sentence bill eliminating the monopoly privileges of the Post Office. He said to me: "You know I agree with you completely, but can you name me an organized group that will come and testify in favor of that bill? I know about the organized groups that will be there to testify against it. There will be the postal employees union; there will be the organization of newspapers and of magazines who will testify against that bill." And he went down the list. All of those organized groups would testify against it. The people who are benefited don't even know that they would be benefited. If you eliminated the monopoly of the Post Office, there would develop a viable active private industry carrying mail. Some of my young students and friends might at some time be employed in such an industry, but do they know it? Are they going to go down to Washington to campaign in favor of that bill? Not a chance of it. "So," he said, "there is not a chance in the world of getting that bill through. It's just a waste of my energy and time to move in that direction."

Many years ago an ex-president of General Motors testified before Congress and was so injudicious as to make the statement that "What's good for General Motors is good for the country." My colleagues at the university hooted and scorned him for such a self-serving statement. But then the next day they were taking airplanes to Washington to testify before Congress that what was good for higher education was good for the country. Was there one among them who saw the irony and the inconsistency?

Each of us separately will try to use the government mechanism to get special benefits for ourselves.

Again, going back to that episode last year before the WIN Program came into force, President Ford had a summit meeting at which people from around the country came together on the subject of inflation. I heard one representative of special interests after another get on the platform and say, "What this country needs to stop inflation is to cut down government spending . . . and the way to cut down government spending is to spend more on me." That was a universal refrain from the farmers, the trade unions, the business delegates, the representatives of the universities.

Here is the fundamental defect of the political mechanism: it is a system of highly weighted voting under which the special interests have great incentive to promote their own interests at the expense of the general public. The benefits are concentrated; the costs are diffused; and you have therefore a bias in the marketplace which leads to ever greater expansion in the scope of the government and ultimately to control over the individual. The way to get elected to Congress or to the presidency is not really to appeal to the general interest. A majority decides, but it is a special kind of majority. The way to get elected is by putting together a coalition of special interests. You go to a group that has 5 percent of the vote and say, "I will vote for what you want if you don't care what else I do." And they say, "Oh, I don't care what else you do." You go on to another 5 percent, and in this way you are well on your way to assembling 51 percent.

The characteristics of the economic market are very different. The fundamental point is the one I mentioned before. In the economic market—the market in which individuals buy and sell from one another—each person gets what he pays for. There is a dollar-for-dollar relationship. Therefore, you have an incentive proportionate to the cost to examine what you are getting. If you are paying out of your own pocket for something and not out of somebody else's pocket, then you have a very strong incentive to see whether you are getting your money's worth. In addition, nobody can get money from you in the economic market unless you agree. There is nobody who can put his hand in your pocket without your permission. In the political market that is the standard way of financing everything. As a consequence, you have in the economic market true individual freedom and a true individual incentive to get what you vote for and, more important, the incentive to find out whether what you are getting is what you voted for and is proportional to the cost to you.

The fundamental problem of Western society, of a society like ours, is that millions and millions of people must cooperate with one another for their daily bread. Fundamentally, there are only two ways in which large groups of people can be induced to cooperate with one another. One way is the method of the army, through force and coercion and direct order. The general tells the colonel, the colonel tells the major, who tells the lieutenant, and so on down to the private. The other way is through voluntary cooperation among people, each of whom is separately pursuing his own interest. In fact, the first method cannot work. The world is simply too complicated: there are too many facts of special time and place for it to be possible to run any complicated system on the basis of direct order. So that, in fact, all systems of cooperation among large groups of people involve a mixture of these two. But it makes an enormous difference what the mixture is. You know, it is like the old German restaurant joke about *Hasenfeffer*—"half horse, half rabbit" (i.e., one horse, one rabbit). The character of our society is fundamentally determined by whether the horse is the political market and the rabbit the economic market or the other way around. Paradoxically, therefore, the situation is that the economic market is a more effective means for achieving political democracy than is a political market.

Let me add one more word on that. When we think of the economic market and the political market we tend to think in narrow terms. We tend to think of the economic market as concerned with the mundane, material things: producing bread or cheese or automobiles or houses. But the principles I have described apply much more broadly. The private market, the economic market, is also the most effective means for doing good. If one goes back to the period in the United States when we had the most unrestricted operation of the free private market, the nineteenth century, it was also the period of the greatest burst of eleemosynary and charitable activity in the history of our country. My own University of Chicago and many of the other colleges and universities of this country were established at that time by the private market arrangement, namely, by voluntary cooperation among people spending their own money for something they themselves believed in: to establish a university or a college. The great system of public libraries (the Carnegie Libraries) was established during that period. That was a period that saw the birth of the private eleemosynary hospital, of the foreign medical missions, of the societies for the prevention of cruelty to animals, and so on. Name a charitable activity, and in almost every case its origins go back to that time. So the private market—what I described as the economic market of voluntary cooperation—is, in my opinion, the most efficient and effective way of doing good as well as the most effective way of organizing economic activity.

America, not unlike other Western societies, is coming to a crossroads. We cannot continue along the road we have been going. In going from 10 percent of the national income being spent by government to 40 percent it was possible to maintain a large element of freedom and individual liberty because it was possible to give large benefits to small groups at small costs spread over many people. But one thing we can be sure of: in the next forty years we cannot go from 40 percent to 60 percent.

At that crossroads is the problem that faced Chile that as a poor country tipped over at 40 percent. Britain is wealthier but appears on the verge of tipping over at 60 percent. We still have some ruin left in us, but pretty soon we are going to be forced to face up to the issue. Where we go from here depends on the new generation that is going to determine the future, on whether in time it comes to recognize that this is a false road which leads to tyranny and misery, not to freedom. Let me propose that as we contemplate that future, we take as our major motto what I would like to see as an eleventh commandment—that everyone shall be free to do good at his own expense.

EIGHT

THE FUTURE OF CAPITALISM

(1977)

When I speak of the future of capitalism, I mean the future of competitive capitalism—a free enterprise capitalism. In a certain sense, every major society is capitalist. Russia has a great deal of capital, but the capital is under the control of governmental officials who are supposedly acting as the agents of the state. That turns capitalism (state capitalism) into a wholly different system than a system under which capital is controlled by individuals in their private capacity as owners and operators of industry. What I want to speak about tonight is the future of private enterprise—of competitive capitalism.

The future of private enterprise capitalism is also the future of a free society. There is no possibility of having a politically free society unless the major part of its economic resources are operated under a capitalistic private enterprise system.

The Trend toward Collectivism

The real question therefore is the future of human freedom. The question that I want to talk about is whether or not we are going to complete the movement that has been going on for the past forty or fifty years, away from a free society and toward a collectivist society. Are we going to continue down that path until we have followed Chile by losing our political freedom and coming under the thumb of an all-powerful government? Or are we going to be able to halt that trend, perhaps even reverse it, and establish a greater degree of freedom?

One thing is clear, we cannot continue along the lines that we have been moving. In 1928, less than fifty years ago, government at all levels—federal, state, and local—spent less than 10 percent of the national income. Two-thirds of that was at the state and local level. Federal spending amounted to less than 3 percent of the national income. Today total government spending at all levels amounts to 40 percent of the national income, and two-thirds of that is at the federal level. So federal government spending has moved in less than fifty years from 3 percent to over 25 percent— total government spending from 10 percent to 40 percent. Now I guarantee you one thing. In the next fifty years government spending cannot move from 40 percent of the national income to 60 percent. (Legislatures have tried to legislate that the value of π shall be exactly three and a seventh, but they cannot repeal the laws of arithmetic!)

We cannot continue on this path. The question is, will we keep trying to continue on this path until we have lost our freedom and turned our lives over to an all-powerful government in Washington, or will we stop?

In judging this possibility, it's worth talking a little bit about where we are and how we got here—about the present and the past. Let me say at the outset that with all the problems I am going to talk about, this still remains a predominantly free society. There is no great country in the world (there are some small enclaves but no great country) that offers as much freedom to the individual as the United States does. But having said that we ought also to recognize how far we have gone away from the ideal of freedom and the extent to which our lives are restricted by governmental enactments.

In talking about freedom it is important at the outset to distinguish two different meanings on the economic level, of the concept of free enterprise, for there is no term that is more misused or misunderstood. The one meaning that is often attached to free enterprise is the meaning that enterprises shall be free to do what they want.

That is not the meaning that has historically been attached to free enterprise. What we really mean by free enterprise is the freedom of individuals to set up enterprises. It is the freedom of an individual to engage in an activity so long as he uses only voluntary methods of getting other individuals to cooperate with him. If you want to see how far we have moved from the basic concept of free enterprise, you can consider how free anyone is to set up an enterprise. You are not free to establish a bank or to go into the taxicab business unless you can get a certificate of convenience and necessity from the local, state, or federal authorities. You cannot become a lawyer or a physician or a plumber or a mortician (and you can name many other cases) unless you can get a license from the government to engage in that activity. You cannot go into the business of delivering the mail or providing electricity or of providing telephone service unless you get a permit from the government to do so. You cannot raise funds on the capital market and get other people to lend you money unless you go through the Securities and Exchange Commission and fill out the four hundred pages of forms that they require. To take the latest restriction on freedom, you cannot any longer engage in voluntary deals with others or make bets with other people about the future prices of commodities unless you get the approval of the government.

Rising Taxation

Another example of the extent to which we have moved away from a free society is the 40 percent of our earnings, on the average, that is co-opted by the government. Each and every one of us works from the first of January to late in April or May in order to pay governmental expenses before we can start to work for our own expenses.

If you want to look at it still another way, the government owns 48 percent of every corporation in the United States. We talk about ourselves as a free enterprise society. Yet in terms of the fundamental question of who owns the means of production, in the corporate sector we are 48 percent socialistic because the corporate tax is 48 percent. What does it mean if I own 1 percent of a corporation? It means I am entitled to 1 percent of the profits and 1 percent of the losses. Well, the federal government shares 48 percent of your profits and 48 percent of your losses (if you have some previous profits to offset against those losses).

Once when I was in Yugoslavia some years ago I calculated that the difference in the degree of socialism in the United States and in communist Yugoslavia was exactly eighteen percentage points, because the US government took 48 percent of the profits of every corporation and the Yugoslav government took 66 percent of the profits of every corporation. And, of course, those numbers grossly understate the role of the government because of its effect in regulating business in areas other than taxation.

Let me give you another example of the extent to which we have lost freedom. About a year or so ago, I had a debate in Washington with that great saint of the United States consumer, Ralph Nader. I planted a question on him because I knew what the answer would be and I wanted to extract the answer. The question I took up was the question of state laws requiring people who ride motorcycles to wear motorcycle helmets. Now I believe in many ways that law is the best litmus paper I know to distinguish true believers in individualism from people who do not believe in individualism because this is the case in which the man riding the motorcycle is risking only his own life. He may be a fool to drive that motorcycle without a helmet. But part of freedom and liberty is the freedom to be a fool! So I expressed the view that the state laws that make it compulsory for people who are riding motorcycles to wear helmets were against individual freedom and against the principles of a free society. I asked Ralph Nader for his opinion, and he gave the answer I expected. He said, "Well, that's all very well for a different society. But you must realize that today, if a motorcyclist driving down the road without a helmet splashes himself on the pavement, a government-subsidized ambulance will come to pick him up, they will take him to a government-subsidized hospital, he will be buried in a government-subsidized cemetery, and his wife and children will be supported by government-subsidized welfare. Therefore we can't let him!" What he was saying was that every single one of us bears on our back a stamp that says "Property of the US Government. Do not fold, bend, or mutilate."

That is essentially the fundamental principle that animates the Ralph Naders of our time—the people who want the power to be in government. You see it everywhere. You see it in a law passed a few years ago that requires the Treasury Department to report to the Congress a category called "Tax expenditures." Tax expenditures are taxes that are not collected from you because of various deductions permitted by the law (such as interest or excess depreciation). The principle is that you are, after all, the property of the US government. You work for the US government, and the US government lets you keep a little of what you earn in order to be sure that it'll keep you working hard for it. But the rest of it is the property of the US government. And if the US government allows you to deduct something from your taxes, it's providing for the expenditure. It's not a right that you have to keep it. It belongs to the government!

Other Freedoms Denied

We have gone very far indeed along the road to losing freedom. But you may say that I am talking only about economic matters, about whether you can enter a profession or an occupation. What about political freedom? What about the freedom of speech? How many businessmen have you heard in the past ten years who have been willing to stand up on some public rostrum and take issue with governmental policies? I have heard many a businessman get up and express general sentiments in favor of free enterprise and of competition. I have heard very few get up and criticize particular measures taken by government. And I don't blame them. They would be fools to do it! Because any businessman who has the nerve to do that has to look over one shoulder and see what the Internal Revenue Service is going to do to his books the next day. And he has to look over the other shoulder to see whether the Justice Department is going to launch an antitrust suit. And then he has to find two or three more shoulders to see what the Federal Trade Commission is going to do. You can take any other three letters of the alphabet and ask what they are going to do to you. In fact, a businessman today does not have effective freedom of speech.

But businessmen don't matter since they're only material business people. What about those people for whom we are really concerned: the intellectuals?

I asked my colleagues, suppose I take a professor from a medical school whose research and training is largely being financed by the National Institutes of Health. Do you suppose he wouldn't think three times before he gives a speech against socialized medicine? Suppose I take one of my colleagues in economics who has been supported by a grant from the National Science Foundation. I personally happen to think there is no justification for the National Science Foundation. (As it happens, I have never received a grant from them though I might have. It isn't that they have turned me down; I haven't asked them!) But nonetheless, do you suppose my colleagues would not be inhibited in speaking out? In fact, I have often said about the only people who have any real freedom of speech left are people who are in the fortunate position of myself: tenured professors at major private universities on the verge of retirement!

Freedom of the Press

Let me give you an even more chilling story about freedom of the press. The other day I got a clipping from an English paper from a friend of mine, indicating that the *London Times* had been prevented from publishing on one day because the unions, who have controlled the press, refused to publish because the issue carried a story that was critical of the policies of unions. Do you mean to say that there aren't American newspapers that would hesitate very much before printing stories and articles that would be regarded as antagonistic by the trade unions on which they depend to produce their papers?

So there is no way of separating economic freedom from political freedom. If you don't have economic freedom, you don't have political freedom. The only way you can have the one is to have the other.

The Nineteenth Century

So much for the present, what about the past? The closest approach to free enterprise we have ever had in the United States was in the nineteenth century. Yet your children will hear over and over again in their schools and in their classes the myth that that was a terrible period when the robber barons were grinding the poor miserable people under their heels. That's a myth constructed out of whole cloth. The plain fact is that never in human history has there been a period when the ordinary man improved his condition and benefited his life as much as he did during that period of the nineteenth century when we had the closest approach to free enterprise that we have ever had. Most of us in this room, I venture to say, are beneficiaries of that period. I speak of myself. My parents came to this country in the 1890s. Like millions of others they came with empty hands. They were able to find a place in this country, to build a life for themselves and to provide a basis on which their children and their children's children could have a better life. There is no saga in history remotely comparable to that of the United States during that era, welcoming millions and millions of people from all over the world and enabling them to find a place for themselves and to improve their lives. And it was possible only because there was an essentially free society.

If the laws and regulations that today hamstring industry and commerce had been in effect in the nineteenth century, our standard of living today would be below that of the nineteenth century. It would have been impossible to have absorbed the millions of people who came to this country.

Why Regimentation?

What produced the shift? Why did we move from a situation in which we had an essentially free society to a situation of increasing regimentation by government? In my opinion the fundamental cause of most government intervention is an unholy coalition between well-meaning people seeking to do good on the one hand and special interests (meaning you and me) on the other taking advantage of those activities for our own purposes.

The great movement toward government has not come about as a result of people with evil intentions trying to do evil. The great growth of government has come about because of good people trying to do good. But the method by which they have tried to do good has been basically flawed. They have tried to do good with other people's money. Doing good with other people's money has two basic flaws. In the first place, you never spend anybody else's money as carefully as you spend your own. So a large fraction of that money is inevitably wasted. In the second place, and equally important, you cannot do good with other people's money unless you first get the money away from them. So that force—sending a policeman to take the money from somebody's pocket—is fundamentally at the basis of the philosophy of the welfare state. That is why the attempt by good people to do good has led to disastrous results. It was this movement toward welfare statism that produced the phenomenon in Chile that ended the Allende regime. It is this tendency to try to do good with other people's money that has brought Great Britain—once the greatest nation of the earth, the nation that is the source of our traditions and our values and our beliefs in a free society—to the edge of catastrophe. It will be touch and go whether over the next five years Great Britain will be able to maintain a free society or relapse into collectivism.

When you start on the road to do good with other people's money, it is easy at first. You've got a lot of people to pay taxes and a small number of people for whom you are trying to do good. But the later stages become harder and harder. As the number of people on the receiving end grows, you end up in the position where you are taxing 50 percent of the people to help 50 percent of the people or, really, 100 percent of the people to distribute benefits to 100 percent! The reductio ad absurdum of this policy is a proposal to send out a rain of $50 checks to all and sundry in the next few months.

The Future

Where do we go from here? People may say, "You can't turn the clock back. How can you go back?" But the thing that always amuses me about that argument is that the people who make it and who accuse me or my colleagues of trying to turn the clock back to the nineteenth century are themselves busily at work trying to turn the clock back to the seventeenth century.

Adam Smith, two hundred years ago, in 1776, wrote *The Wealth of Nations.* It was an attack on the government controls of his time—on mercantilism, on tariffs, on restrictions, on governmental monopoly. But those are exactly the results that the present-day reformers are seeking to achieve.

In any event, that's a foolish question. The real question is not whether you are turning the clock back or forward but whether you are doing the right thing? Do you mean to say you should never learn from your mistakes?

Some people argue that technological changes require big government and that you can no longer talk in the terms of the nineteenth century when the government only absorbed 3 percent of the national income. You have to have big government because of these technological changes. That's nonsense from beginning to end. Some technological changes no doubt require the government to engage in activities different from those in which it engaged before. But other technological changes *reduce* the need for government. The improvements in communication and transportation have greatly reduced the possibility of local monopoly, which requires government intervention to protect the consumers. Moreover, if you look at the record the great growth of government has not been in the areas dictated by technological change. The great growth of government has been to take money from some people and to give it to others. The only way technology has entered into that is by providing the computers that make it possible to do so.

Other people will say, how can you talk about stopping this trend? What about big business? Does it really make any difference whether automobiles are made by General Motors, which is an enormous bureaucratic enterprise employing thousands of people, or whether they are made by an agency of the United States government, which is another bureaucratic enterprise?

The answer to that is very simple. It makes all the difference in the world because there is a fundamental difference between the two. There is no way in which General Motors can get a dollar from you unless you agree to give it to the company. That's a voluntary exchange. It can only get money from you by providing you with something you value more than the money you give it. If it tries to force something on you that you don't want, ask Mr. Henry Ford what happened when Ford tried to introduce the Edsel. On the other hand the government can get money from you without your consent. They can send policemen to take it out of your pocket. General Motors doesn't have that power. And that is all the difference in the world. It is the difference between a society in which exchange is voluntary and a society in which exchange is not voluntary. It's the reason why the government, when it is in the saddle, produces poor quality at high cost, while industry, when it's in the saddle, produces quality at low cost. The one has to satisfy its customers and the other does not.

Two Possible Scenarios

Where shall we go from here? There are two possible scenarios. The one (and I very much fear it's the more likely) is that we will continue in the direction in which we have been going, with gradual increases in the scope of government and government control.

If we do continue in that direction, two results are inevitable. One result is financial crisis and the other is a loss of freedom.

The example of England is a frightening example to contemplate. England has been moving in this direction. We're about twenty years behind England in this motion. But England was moving in this direction earlier than we were moving and has moved much farther. The effects are patent and clear. But at least when England moved in this direction and thus lost its power politically and internationally, the United States was there to take over the defense of the free world. But I ask you, when the United States follows that direction, who is going to take over from us? That's one scenario, and I very much fear it's the more likely one.

The other scenario is that we will, in fact, halt this trend, that we will call a halt to the apparently increasing growth of government, set a limit, and hold it back.

There are many favorable signs from this point of view. I may say that the greatest reason for hope, in my opinion, is the inefficiency of government. Many people complain about government waste. I welcome it. I welcome it for two reasons. In the first place, efficiency is not a desirable thing if somebody is doing a bad thing. A great teacher of mine, a mathematical economist, once wrote an article on the teaching of statistics. He said, "Pedagogical ability is a vice rather than a virtue if it is devoted to teaching error." That's a fundamental principle. Government is doing things that we don't want it to do, so the more money it wastes the better.

In the second place, waste brings home to the public at large the fact that government is not an efficient and effective instrument for achieving its objectives. One of the great causes for hope is a growing disillusionment around the country with the idea that government is the all-wise, all-powerful big brother who can solve every problem that comes along, that if only you throw enough money at a problem it will be resolved.

Several years ago John Kenneth Galbraith wrote an article in which he said that New York City had no problem that could not be solved by an increase in government spending in New York. Well, since that time the budget in the City of New York has more than doubled and so have the problems of New York. The one is cause and the other effect. The government has spent more but that meant that the people have less to spend. Since the government spends money less efficiently than individuals spend their own money, as government spending has gone up the problems have gotten worse. My main point is that this inefficiency, this waste, brings home to the public at large the undesirability of governmental intervention. I believe that a major source of hope is in the widespread rise in the tide of feeling that government is not the appropriate way to solve our problems.

There are also many unfavorable signs. It's far easier to enact laws than to repeal them. Every special interest, including you and me, has great resistance to giving up its special privileges. I remember when Gerald Ford became president and he called a summit conference to do something about the problems of inflation. I sat at that summit conference and heard representatives of one group after another go to the podium—a representative of business, a representative of the farmers, a representative of labor, you name the group—they all went to the podium and they all said the same thing. They said, "Of course, we recognize that in order to stop inflation, we must cut down government spending. And I tell you the way to cut down government spending is to spend more on me." That was the universal refrain.

Many people say that one of the causes for hope is the rising recognition by the business community that business enterprise is a threat to the free enterprise system. I wish I could believe that, but I do not. You must recognize the facts. Business corporations in general are not a defense of free enterprise. On the contrary, they are one of the chief sources of danger.

The two greatest enemies of free enterprise in the United States, in my opinion, have been, on the one hand, my fellow intellectuals and, on the other hand, the business corporations of this country. They are enemies for opposite reasons. Every one of my fellow intellectuals believes in freedom for himself. He wants free speech. He wants free research. I ask him, "Isn't this a terrible waste that a dozen people are studying the same problem? Oughtn't we to have a central planning committee to decide what research projects various individuals are to undertake?" He'll look at me as if I'm crazy, and he'll say, "What do you mean? Don't you understand about the value of academic freedom and freedom of research and duplication?" But when it comes to business he says, "Oh, that's wasteful competition. That's duplication over there! We must have a central planning board to make those things intelligent, sensible!"

So every intellectual is in favor of freedom for himself and against freedom for anybody else. The businessman and the business enterprise are very different. Every businessman and every business enterprise is in favor of freedom for everybody else, but when it comes to himself, that's a different question. We have to have that tariff to protect us against competition from abroad. We have to have that special provision in the tax code. We have to have that subsidy. Businessmen are in favor of freedom for everybody else but not for themselves.

There are many notable exceptions. There are many business leaders who have been extremely farsighted in their understanding of the problem and will come to the defense of a free enterprise system. But for the business community in general, the tendency is to take out advertisements, such as the US Steel Company taking out full-page ads to advertise the virtues of free enterprise but then to plead before Congress for an import quota on steel from Japan. The only result of that is for everybody who is fair-minded to say, "What a bunch of hypocrites!" And they're right.

Now don't misunderstand me, I don't blame business enterprise. I don't blame US Steel for seeking to get those special privileges. The managers of US Steel have an obligation to their stockholders, and they would be false to that obligation if they did not try to take advantage of the opportunities to get assistance. I don't blame them. I blame the rest of us for letting them get away with it. We must recognize what the real problem is and recognize that that is not a source of strength.

Faith in the Future

Where are we going to end up? I do not know. I think that depends upon a great many things.

I am reminded of a story that will illustrate what we may need. It has to do with a young and attractive nun who was driving a car down a superhighway and ran out of gas. She remembered that a mile back there had been a gas station. She got out of her car, hiked up her habit, and walked back to the gas station. When she got to the station, she found that there was only one young man in attendance there. He said he'd love to help her but couldn't leave the gas station because he was the only one there. He said he would try to find a container in which he could give her some gas. He hunted around the gas station and couldn't find a decent container. The only thing he could find was a little baby's potty that had been left there. So he filled the baby potty with gasoline and gave it to the nun. She took the baby potty and walked the mile down the road to her car. She got to her car and opened the gas tank and started to pour it in. Just at that moment a great big Cadillac came barreling down the road at eighty miles an hour. The driver was looking out and couldn't believe what he was seeing. So he jammed on his brakes, stopped, backed up, opened the window, and looked out and said, "Sister, I only wish I had such faith!"

Finally, may I say a word of congratulations to Pepperdine University, especially the associates, for your ability not only to survive but to flourish in an educational world increasingly dominated by government institutions. Unless this trend can be contained, or even better reversed, by the continued existence and growth of private institutions like Pepperdine University and my own University of Chicago, our free society will be in mortal danger. Thank you.

Note

The founding four hundred members of the Pepperdine University Associates assembled for the first time on February 9, 1977, to celebrate the fortieth anniversary of the university and to hear the charter address, "The Future of Capitalism," by Milton Friedman.

NINE

FAIR VERSUS FREE

(1977)

In presenting his energy program, President Carter stressed "fairness" as an essential ingredient of an acceptable program. The Federal Communications Commission seeks to enforce a "fairness doctrine" on radio and TV stations. We suffered numerous "fair trade" laws until they were declared unenforceable. One businessman vies with another in proclaiming his faith in competition—provided that it is "fair."

Yet scrutinize word for word the Declaration of Independence, the Constitution, and the Bill of Rights and you will not find the word "fair." The First Amendment does not protect the fair exercise of religion, but the free exercise thereof; it does not restrain Congress from abridging the fairness of speech or of the press but the freedom of speech or of the press.

The modern tendency to substitute fair for free reveals how far we have moved from the initial conception of the Founding Fathers. They viewed government as policeman and umpire. They sought to establish a framework within which individuals could pursue their own objectives in their own way, separately or through voluntary cooperation, provided only that they did not interfere with the freedom of others to do likewise.

The modern conception is very different. Government has become big brother. Its function has become to protect the citizen not merely from his fellows, but from himself, whether he wants to be protected or not. Government is not simply an umpire but an active participant, entering into every nook and cranny of social and economic activity. All this is in order to promote the high-minded goals of fairness, justice, and equality.

Does this not constitute progress? A move toward a more humane society? Quite the contrary. When fairness replaces freedom, all our liberties are in danger. In *Walden,* Thoreau says, "If I knew for a certainty that a man was coming to my house with the conscious design of doing me good, I should run for my life." That is the way I feel when I hear my "servants" in Washington assuring me of the fairness of their edicts.

There is no objective standard of fairness. Fairness is strictly in the eye of the beholder. If speech must be fair, then it cannot also be free; someone must decide what is fair. A radio station is not free to transmit unfair speech as judged by the bureaucrats at the Federal Communications Commission. If the printed press were subject to a comparable fairness doctrine, it too would have to be controlled by a government bureau, and our vaunted free press would soon become a historical curiosity.

What is true for speech—where the conflict is perhaps clearest—is equally true for every other area. To a producer or seller, a fair price is a high price. To the buyer or consumer, a fair price is a low price. How is the conflict to be adjudicated? By competition in a free market? or by government bureaucrats in a fair market?

Businessmen who sing the glories of free enterprise and then demand fair competition are enemies, not friends, of free markets. To them, fair competition is a euphemism for a price-fixing agreement. They are exemplifying Adam Smith's remark that "People of the same trade seldom meet together, even for merriment and diversion, but the conversation ends in a conspiracy against the public, or in some contrivance to raise prices." For consumers, the more unfair the competition the better, for that assures lowest prices and highest quality.

Is then the search for fairness all a mistake? Not at all. There is a real role for fairness, but that role is in constructing general rules and adjudicating disputes about the rules, not in determining the outcome of our separate activities. That is the sense in which we speak of a fair game and a fair umpire. If we applied the present doctrine of fairness to a football game, the referee would be required after each play to move the ball backward or forward enough to make sure that the game ended in a draw!

Our Founding Fathers designed a fair Constitution to protect human freedom. In Thomas Jefferson's ringing phrases from the Declaration of Independence, "Governments are instituted among Men ... to secure ... certain unalienable Rights, that among these are Life, Liberty, and the Pursuit of Happiness."

TEN

CREATED EQUAL

(1980)

"Equality, liberty"—what precisely do these words from the Declaration of Independence mean? Can the ideals they express be realized in practice? Are equality and liberty consistent one with the other or are they in conflict?

Since well before the Declaration of Independence, these questions have played a central role in the history of the United States. The attempt to answer them has shaped the intellectual climate of opinion, led to bloody wars, and produced major changes in economic and political institutions. This attempt continues to dominate our political debate. It will shape our future as it has our past.

In the early decades of the Republic, equality meant equality before God; liberty meant the liberty to shape one's own life. The obvious conflict between the Declaration of Independence and the institution of slavery occupied the center of the stage. That conflict was finally resolved by the Civil War. The debate then moved to a different level. Equality came more and more to be interpreted as "equality of opportunity" in the sense that no one should be prevented by arbitrary obstacles from using his capacities to pursue his own objectives. That is still its dominant meaning to most citizens of the United States.

Neither equality before God nor equality of opportunity presented any conflict with liberty to shape one's own life. Quite the opposite. Equality and liberty were two faces of the same basic value—that every individual should be regarded as an end in himself.

A very different meaning of equality has emerged in the United States in recent decades—equality of outcome. Everyone should have the same level of living or of income, should finish the race at the same time. Equality of outcome is in clear conflict with liberty. The attempt to promote it has been a major source of bigger and bigger government and of government-imposed restrictions on our liberty.

Equality Before God

When Thomas Jefferson, at the age of thirty-three, wrote "all men are created equal," he and his contemporaries did not take these words literally. They did not regard men—or as we would say today, persons—as equal in physical characteristics, emotional reactions, mechanical and intellectual abilities. Thomas Jefferson himself was a most remarkable person. At the age of twenty-six he designed his beautiful house at Monticello (Italian for "little mountain"), supervised its construction, and, indeed, is said to have done some of the work himself. In the course of his life, he was an inventor, a scholar, an author, a statesman, governor of the State of Virginia, president of the United States, minister to France, founder of the University of Virginia—hardly an average man.

The clue to what Thomas Jefferson and his contemporaries meant by equal is seen in the next phrase of the Declaration—"endowed by their Creator with certain unalienable rights; that among these are Life, Liberty, and the pursuit of Happiness." Men were equal before God. Each person is precious in and of himself. He has unalienable rights, rights that no one else is entitled to invade. He is entitled to serve his own purposes and not to be treated simply as an instrument to promote someone else's purposes. "Liberty" is part of the definition of equality, not in conflict with it.

Equality before God—personal equality[1]—is important precisely because people are not identical. Their different values, their different tastes, their different capacities will lead them to want to lead very different lives. Personal equality requires respect for their right to do so, not the imposition on them of someone else's values or judgment. Jefferson had no doubt that some men were superior to others, that there was an elite. But that did not give them the right to rule others.

If an elite did not have the right to impose its will on others, neither did any other group, even a majority. Every person was to be his own ruler—provided that he did not interfere with the similar right of others. Government was established to protect that right—from fellow citizens and from external threat—not to give a majority unbridled rule. Jefferson had three achievements he wanted to be remembered for inscribed on his tombstone: the Virginia statute for religious freedom (a precursor of the US Bill of Rights designed to protect minorities against domination by majorities), authorship of the Declaration of Independence, and the founding of the University of Virginia. The goal of the framers of the Constitution of the United States, drafted by Jefferson's contemporaries, was a national government strong enough to defend the country and promote the general welfare but at the same time sufficiently limited in power to protect the individual citizen, and the separate state governments, from domination by the national government. Democratic, in the sense of widespread participation in government, yes; in the political sense of majority rule, clearly no.

Similarly, Alexis de Tocqueville, the famous French political philosopher and sociologist, in his classic *Democracy in America,* written after a lengthy visit in the 1830s, saw equality, not majority rule, as the outstanding characteristic of America. "In America," he wrote,

> the aristocratic element has always been feeble from its birth; and if at the present day it is not actually destroyed, it is at any rate so completely disabled, that we can scarcely assign to it any degree of influence on the course of affairs. The democratic principle, on the contrary, has gained so much strength by time, by events, and by legislation, as to have become not only predominant but all-powerful. There is no family or corporate authority. . . .

> America, then, exhibits in her social state a most extraordinary phenomenon. Men are there seen on a greater equality in point of fortune and intellect, or, in other words, more equal in their strength, than in any other country of the world, or in any age of which history has preserved the remembrance.[2]

Tocqueville admired much of what he observed, but he was by no means an uncritical admirer, fearing that democracy carried too far might undermine civic virtue. As he put it, "There is . . . a manly and lawful passion for equality which incites men to wish all to be powerful and honored. This passion tends to elevate the humble to the rank of the great; but there exists also in the human heart a depraved taste for equality, which impels the weak to attempt to lower the powerful to their own level, and reduces men to prefer equality in slavery to inequality with freedom."[3]

It is striking testimony to the changing meaning of words that in recent decades the Democratic Party of the United States has been the chief instrument for strengthening that government power that Jefferson and many of his contemporaries viewed as the greatest threat to democracy. And it has striven to increase government power in the name of a concept of "equality" that is almost the opposite of the concept of equality Jefferson identified with liberty and Tocqueville with democracy.

Of course the practice of the Founding Fathers did not always correspond to their preaching. The most obvious conflict was slavery. Thomas Jefferson himself owned slaves until the day he died—July 4, 1826. He agonized repeatedly about slavery, suggested in his notes and correspondence plans for eliminating slavery, but never publicly proposed any such plans or campaigned against the institution.

Yet the Declaration he drafted had either to be blatantly violated by the nation he did so much to create and form or slavery had to be abolished. Little wonder that the early decades of the Republic saw a rising tide of controversy about the institution of slavery. That controversy ended in a Civil War that, in the words of Abraham Lincoln's Gettysburg Address, tested whether a "nation, conceived in liberty and dedicated to the proposition that all men are created equal . . . can long endure." The nation endured but only at a tremendous cost in lives, property, and social cohesion.

Equality of Opportunity

Once the Civil War abolished slavery and the concept of personal equality—equality before God and the law—came closer to realization, emphasis shifted, in intellectual discussion and in government and private policy, to a different concept—equality of opportunity.

Literal equality of opportunity—in the sense of identity—is impossible. One child is born blind, another with sight. One child has parents deeply concerned about his welfare who provide a background of culture and understanding; another has dissolute, improvident parents. One child is born in the United States, another in India or China or Russia. They clearly do not have identical opportunities open to them at birth, and there is no way that their opportunities can be made identical.

Like personal equality, equality of opportunity is not to be interpreted literally. Its real meaning is perhaps best expressed by the French expression dating from the French Revolution: *Une carrière ouverte aux les talents*—a career open to the talents. No arbitrary obstacles should prevent people from achieving those positions for which their talents fit them and for which their values lead them to seek. Not birth, nationality, color, religion, sex, or any other irrelevant characteristic should determine the opportunities that are open to a person—only his abilities.

On this interpretation, equality of opportunity simply spells out in more detail the meaning of personal equality, of equality before the law. And like personal equality, it has meaning and importance precisely because people are different in their genetic and cultural characteristics and hence both want to and can pursue different careers.

Equality of opportunity, like personal equality, is not inconsistent with liberty; on the contrary, it is an essential component of liberty. If some people are denied access to particular positions in life for which they are qualified simply because of their ethnic background, color, or religion, that is an interference with their right to "Life, Liberty, and the pursuit of Happiness." It denies equality of opportunity and, by the same token, sacrifices the freedom of some for the advantage of others.

Like every ideal, equality of opportunity is incapable of being fully realized. The most serious departure was undoubtedly with respect to the blacks, particularly in the South but in the North as well. Yet there was also tremendous progress for blacks and for other groups. The very concept of a melting pot reflected the goal of equality of opportunity. So also did the expansion of free education at elementary, secondary, and higher levels, though this development has not been an unmixed blessing.

The priority given to equality of opportunity in the hierarchy of values generally accepted by the public after the Civil War is manifested particularly in economic policy. The catchwords were free enterprise, competition, laissez-faire. Everyone was to be free to go into any business, follow any occupation, buy any property, subject only to the agreement of the other parties to the transaction. Each was to have the opportunity to reap the benefits if he succeeded, to suffer the costs if he failed. There were to be no arbitrary obstacles. Performance, not birth, religion, or nationality, was the touchstone.

One corollary was the development of what many who regarded themselves as the cultural elite sneered at as vulgar materialism—an emphasis on the almighty dollar, on wealth as both the symbol and the seal of success. As Tocqueville pointed out, this emphasis reflected the unwillingness of the community to accept the traditional criteria in feudal and aristocratic societies, namely, birth and parentage. Performance was the obvious alternative, and the accumulation of wealth was the most readily available measure of performance.

Another corollary, of course, was an enormous release of human energy that made America an increasingly productive and dynamic society in which social mobility was an everyday reality. Still another, perhaps surprisingly, was an explosion in charitable activity. This explosion was made possible by the rapid growth in wealth. It took the form it did—of nonprofit hospitals, privately endowed colleges and universities, a plethora of charitable organizations directed to helping the poor—because of the dominant values of the society, including, especially, promotion of equality of opportunity.

Of course, in the economic sphere as elsewhere, practice did not always conform to the ideal. Government *was* kept to a minor role; no major obstacles to enterprise were erected; and, by the end of the nineteenth century, positive government measures, especially the Sherman Anti-Trust Law, were adopted to eliminate private barriers to competition. But extralegal arrangements continued to interfere with the freedom of individuals to enter various businesses or professions, and social practices unquestionably gave special advantages to persons born in the "right" families, of the "right" color, and of the "right" religion. However, the rapid rise in the economic and social position of various less privileged groups demonstrates that these obstacles were by no means insurmountable.

In respect of government measures, one major deviation from free markets was in foreign trade, where Alexander Hamilton's *Report on Manufactures* had enshrined tariff protection for domestic industries as part of the American way. Tariff protection was inconsistent with thoroughgoing equality of opportunity and, indeed, with the free immigration of persons, which was the rule until World War I, except Orientals. Yet it could be rationalized both by the needs of national defense and on the very different ground that equality stops at the water's edge—an illogical rationalization that is adopted also by most of today's proponents of a very different concept of equality.

Equality of Outcome

That different concept, equality of outcome, has been gaining ground in this century. It first affected government policy in Great Britain and on the European continent. Over the past half-century it has increasingly affected government policy in the United States as well. In some intellectual circles the desirability of equality of outcome has become an article of religious faith: everyone should finish the race at the same time. As the Dodo said in *Alice in Wonderland,* "*Everybody* has won, and *all* must have prizes."

For this concept, as for the other two, equal is not to be interpreted literally as identical. No one really maintains that everyone, regardless of age or sex or other physical attributes, should have identical rations of each separate item of food, clothing, and so on. The goal is rather fairness, a much vaguer notion—indeed, one that it is difficult, if not impossible, to define precisely. "Fair shares for all" is the modern slogan that has replaced Karl Marx's, "To each according to his needs, from each according to his ability."

This concept of equality differs radically from the other two. Government measures that promote personal equality or equality of opportunity enhance liberty; government measures to achieve fair shares for all reduce liberty. If what people get is to be determined by fairness, who is to decide what is fair? As a chorus of voices asked the Dodo, "But who is to give the prizes?" Fairness is not an objectively determined concept once it departs from identity. Fairness, like needs, is in the eye of the beholder. If all are to have fair shares, someone or some group of people must decide what shares are fair—and they must be able to impose their decisions on others, taking from those who have more than their fair share and giving to those who have less. Are those who make and impose such decisions equal to those for whom they decide? Are we not in George Orwell's *Animal Farm,* where "all animals are equal, but some animals are more equal than others"?

In addition, if what people get is determined by fairness and not by what they produce, where are the prizes to come from? What incentive is there to work and produce? How is it to be decided who is to be the doctor, who the lawyer, who the garbage collector, who the street sweeper? What assures that people will accept the roles assigned to them and then carry out those roles in accordance with their abilities? Clearly, only force or the threat of force will work.

The key point is not merely that practice will depart from the ideal. Of course it will, as it does with respect to the other two concepts of equality as well. The point is rather that there is a fundamental conflict between the *ideal* of fair shares, or of its precursor, "to each according to his needs," and the *ideal* of personal liberty. This conflict has plagued every attempt to make equality of outcome the overriding principle of social organization. The end result has invariably been a state of terror: Russia, China, and, more recently, Cambodia offer clear and convincing evidence. And even terror has not equalized outcomes. In every case, wide inequality persists by any criterion; inequality between the rulers and the ruled, not only in power but also in material standards of life.[4]

The far less extreme measures taken in Western countries in the name of equality of outcome have shared the same fate to a lesser extent. They, too, have restricted individual liberty. They, too, have failed to achieve their objective. It has proved impossible to define fair shares in a way that is generally acceptable or to satisfy the members of the community that they are being treated fairly. On the contrary, dissatisfaction has mounted with every additional attempt to implement equality of outcome.

Much of the moral fervor behind the drive for equality of outcome comes from the widespread belief that it is not fair that some children should have a great advantage over others simply because they happen to have wealthy parents. Of course it is not fair. However, unfairness can take many forms. It can take the form of the inheritance of property—bonds and stocks, houses, factories; it can also take the form of the inheritance of talent—musical ability, strength, mathematical genius. The inheritance of property can be interfered with more readily than the inheritance of talent. But from an ethical point of view, is there any difference between the two? Yet many people resent the inheritance of property but not the inheritance of talent.

Look at the same issue from the point of view of the parent. If you want to assure your child a higher income in life, you can do so in various ways. You can buy him (or her) an education that will equip him to pursue an occupation yielding a high income; or you can set him up in a business that will yield a higher income than he could earn as a salaried employee; or you can leave him property, the income from which will enable him to live better. Is there any ethical difference among these three ways of using your property? Or again, if the state leaves you any money to spend over and above taxes, should the state permit you to spend it on riotous living but not to leave it to your children?

The ethical issues involved are subtle and complex. They are not to be resolved by such simplistic formulas as fair shares for all. Indeed, if we took that seriously, youngsters with less musical skill should be given the greatest amount of musical training in order to compensate for their inherited disadvantage and those with greater musical aptitude should be prevented from having access to good musical training, similarly with all other categories of inherited personal qualities. That might be fair to the youngsters lacking in talent, but would it be fair to the talented, let alone to those who had to work to pay for training the youngsters lacking talent or to the persons deprived of the benefits that might have come from the cultivation of the talents of the gifted?

Life is not fair. It is tempting to believe that government can rectify what nature has spawned. But it is also important to recognize how much we benefit from the very unfairness we deplore. There's nothing fair about Marlene Dietrich's having been born with beautiful legs that we all want to look at or about Muhammad Ali's having been born with the skill that made him a great fighter. But on the other side, millions of people who have enjoyed looking at Marlene Dietrich's legs or watching one of Muhammad Ali's fights have benefited from nature's unfairness in producing a Marlene Dietrich and a Muhammad Ali. What kind of a world would it be if everyone were a duplicate of everyone else?

It is certainly not fair that Muhammad Ali should be able to earn millions of dollars in one night. But wouldn't it have been even more unfair to the people who enjoyed watching him if, in the pursuit of some abstract ideal of equality, Muhammad Ali had not been permitted to earn more for one night's fight—or for each day spent in preparing for a fight—than the lowest man on the totem pole could get for a day's unskilled work on the docks? It might have been possible to do that, but the result would have been to deny people the opportunity to watch Muhammad Ali. We doubt very much that he would have been willing to undergo the arduous regimen of training that preceded his fights or to subject himself to the kind of fights he has had, if he were limited to the pay of an unskilled dockworker.

Still another facet of this complex issue of fairness can be illustrated by considering a game of chance, for example, an evening at baccarat. The people who choose to play may start the evening with equal piles of chips, but as the play progresses, those piles will become unequal. By the end of the evening, some will be big winners, others big losers. In the name of the ideal of equality, should the winners be required to repay the losers? That would take all the fun out of the game. Not even the losers would like that. They might like it for the one evening, but would they come back again to play if they knew that, whatever happened, they'd end up exactly where they started?

This example has a great deal more to do with the real world than one might at first suppose. Every day each of us makes decisions that involve taking a chance. Occasionally it's a big chance—as when we decide what occupation to pursue, whom to marry, whether to buy a house or make a major investment. More often it's a small chance, as when we decide what movie to go to, whether to cross the street against the traffic, whether to buy one security rather than another. Each time the question is who is to decide what chances we take? That in turn depends on who bears the consequences of the decision. If we bear the consequences, we can make the decision. But if someone else bears the consequences, should we or will we be permitted to make the decision? If you play baccarat as an agent for someone else with his money, will he, or should he, permit you unlimited scope for decision making? Is he not almost certain to set some limit to your discretion? Will he not lay down some rules for you to observe? To take a very different example, if the government (i.e., your fellow taxpayers) assumes the costs of flood damage to your house, can you be permitted to decide freely whether to build your house on a floodplain? It is no accident that increasing government intervention into personal decisions has gone hand in hand with the drive for fair shares for all.

The system under which people can make their own choices—and bear most of the consequences of their decisions—is the system that has prevailed for most of our history. It is the system that gave the Henry Fords, the Thomas Alva Edisons, the George Eastmans, the John D. Rockefellers, the James Cash Penneys the incentive to transform our society over the past two centuries. It is the system that gave other people an incentive to furnish venture capital to finance the risky enterprises that these ambitious inventors and captains of industry undertook. Of course, there were many losers along the way—probably more losers than winners. We don't remember their names. But for the most part they went in with their eyes open. They knew they were taking chances. And win or lose, society as a whole benefited from their willingness to take a chance.

The fortunes that this system produced came overwhelmingly from developing new products or services or new ways of producing products or services or of distributing them widely. The resulting addition to the wealth of the community as a whole, to the well-being of the masses of the people, amounted to many times the wealth accumulated by the innovators. Henry Ford acquired a great fortune. The country acquired a cheap and reliable means of transportation and the techniques of mass production. Moreover, in many cases the private fortunes were largely devoted in the end to the benefit of society. The Rockefeller, Ford, and Carnegie Foundations are only the most prominent of the numerous private benefactions that are so wonderful as a consequence of the operation of a system that corresponded to "equality of opportunity" and "liberty" as these terms were understood until recently.

One limited sample may give the flavor of the outpouring of philanthropic activity in the nineteenth and early twentieth century. In a book devoted to "cultural philanthropy in Chicago from the 1880s to 1917," Helen Horowitz writes:

> At the turn of the century, Chicago was a city of contradictory impulses: it was both a commercial center dealing in the basic commodities of an industrial society and a community caught in the winds of cultural uplift. As one commentator put it, the city was "a strange combination of pork and Plato."
>
> A major manifestation of Chicago's drive toward culture was the establishment of the city's great cultural institutions in the 1880s and early 1890s (the Art Institute, the Newberry Library, the Chicago Symphony Orchestra, the University of Chicago, the Field Museum, the Crerar Library). . . .
>
> These institutions were a new phenomenon in the city. Whatever the initial impetus behind their founding, they were largely organized, sustained, and controlled by a group of businessmen. . . . Yet while privately supported and managed, the institutions were designed for the whole city. Their trustees had turned to cultural philanthropy not so much to satisfy personal aesthetic or scholarly yearnings as to accomplish social goals. Disturbed by social forces they could not control and filled with idealistic notions of culture, these businessmen saw in the museum, the library, the symphony orchestra, and the university a way to purify their city and to generate a civic renaissance.[5]

Philanthropy was by no means restricted to cultural institutions. There was, as Horowitz writes in another connection, "a kind of explosion of activity on many different levels." And Chicago was not an isolated case. Rather, as Horowitz puts it, "Chicago seemed to epitomize America."[6] The same period saw the establishment of Hull House in Chicago under Jane Addams, the first of many settlement houses established throughout the nation to spread culture and education among the poor and to assist them in their daily problems. Many hospitals, orphanages, and other charitable agencies were set up in the same period.

There is no inconsistency between a free market system and the pursuit of broad social and cultural goals or between a free market system and compassion for the less fortunate, whether that compassion takes the form, as it did in the nineteenth century, of private charitable activity or, as it has done increasingly in the twentieth, of assistance through government—provided that in both cases it is an expression of a desire to help others. There is all the difference in the world, however, between two kinds of assistance through government that seem superficially similar: first, 90 percent of us agreeing to impose taxes on ourselves in order to help the bottom 10 percent and, second, 80 percent voting to impose taxes on the top 10 percent to help the bottom 10 percent—William Graham Sumner's famous example of B and C deciding what D shall do for A.[7] The first may be wise or unwise, an effective or an ineffective way to help the disadvantaged—but it is consistent with belief in both equality of opportunity and liberty. The second seeks equality of outcome and is entirely antithetical to liberty.

Who Favors Equality of Outcome?

There is little support for the goal of equality of outcome despite the extent to which it has become almost an article of religious faith among intellectuals and despite its prominence in the speeches of politicians and the preambles of legislation. The talk

153

is belied alike by the behavior of government, of the intellectuals who most ardently espouse egalitarian sentiments, and of the public at large.

For government, one obvious example is the policy toward lotteries and gambling. New York State—and particularly New York City—is widely and correctly regarded as a stronghold of egalitarian sentiment. Yet the New York State government conducts lotteries and provides facilities for off-track betting on races. It advertises extensively to induce its citizens to buy lottery tickets and bet on the races—at terms that yield a very large profit to the government. At the same time it tries to suppress the numbers game, which, as it happens, offers better odds than the government lottery (especially when account is taken of the greater ease of avoiding tax on winnings). Great Britain, a stronghold, if not the birthplace, of egalitarian sentiment, permits private gambling clubs and betting on races and other sporting events. Indeed, wagering is a national pastime and a major source of government income.

For intellectuals, the clearest evidence is their failure to practice what so many of them preach. Equality of outcome can be promoted on a do-it-yourself basis. First, decide exactly what you mean by equality. Do you want to achieve equality within the United States? in a selected group of countries as a whole? in the world as a whole? Is equality to be judged in terms of income per person, per family, per year, per decade, per lifetime, income in the form of money alone? Or including such nonmonetary items as the rental value of an owned home; food grown for one's own use; services rendered by members of the family not employed for money, notably the housewife? How are physical and mental handicaps or advantages to be allowed for?

However you decide these issues, you can, if you are an egalitarian, estimate what money income would correspond to your concept of equality. If your actual income is higher than that, you can keep that amount and distribute the rest to people who are below that level. If your criterion were to encompass the world—as most egalitarian rhetoric suggests it should—something less than, say, $200 a year (in 1979 dollars) per person would be an amount that would correspond to the conception of equality that seems implicit in most egalitarian rhetoric. That is about the average income per person worldwide.

What Irving Kristol has called the "new class"—government bureaucrats, academics whose research is supported by government funds or who are employed in government-financed think tanks, staffs of the many so-called general interest or public policy groups, journalists and others in the communications industry—are among the most ardent preachers of the doctrine of equality. Yet they remind us very much of the old, if unfair, saw about the Quakers: "They came to the New World to do good and ended up doing well." The members of the new class are in general among the highest paid persons in the community. And for many among them, preaching equality and promoting or administering the resulting legislation has proved an effective means of achieving such high incomes. All of us find it easy to identify our own welfare with the welfare of the community.

Of course, an egalitarian may protest that he is but a drop in the ocean, that he would be willing to redistribute the excess of his income over his concept of an equal income if everyone else were compelled to do the same. On one level this contention that compulsion would change matters is wrong; even if everyone else did the same, his specific contribution to the income of others would still be a drop in the ocean. His individual contribution would be just as large if he were the only contributor as if he were one of many. Indeed it would be more valuable because he could target his contribution to go to the very worst off among those he regards as appropriate recipients. On another level compulsion would change matters drastically; the kind of society that would emerge if such acts of redistribution were voluntary is altogether different—and, by our standards, infinitely preferable—to the kind that would emerge if redistribution were compulsory.

Persons who believe that a society of enforced equality is preferable can also practice what they preach. They can join one of the many communes in this country and elsewhere or establish new ones. And, of course, it is entirely consistent with a belief in personal equality or equality of opportunity and liberty that any group of individuals who wish to live in that way should be free to do so. Our thesis that support for equality of outcome is word-deep receives strong support from the small number of persons who have wished to join such communes and from the fragility of the communes that have been established.

Egalitarians in the United States may object that the fewness of communes and their fragility reflect the opprobrium that a predominantly capitalist society visits on such communes and the resulting discrimination to which they are subjected. That may be true for the United States but as Robert Nozick[8] has pointed out, there is one country where that is not true, where, on the contrary, egalitarian communes are highly regarded and prized. That country is Israel. The kibbutz played a major role in early Jewish settlement in Palestine and continues to play an important role in the state of Israel. A disproportionate fraction of the leaders of the Israeli state were drawn from the kibbutzim. Far from being a source of disapproval, membership in a kibbutz confers social status and commands approbation. Everyone is free to join or leave a kibbutz, and kibbutzim have been viable social organizations. Yet at no time, and certainly not today, have more than about 5 percent of the Jewish population of Israel chosen to be members of a kibbutz. That percentage can be regarded as an upper estimate of the fraction of people who would voluntarily choose a system enforcing equality of outcome in preference to a system characterized by inequality, diversity, and opportunity.

Public attitudes about graduated income taxes are more mixed. Recent referenda on the introduction of graduated state income taxes in some states that do not have them, and on an increase in the extent of graduation in other states, have generally been defeated. On the other hand, the federal income tax is highly graduated, at least on paper, though it also contains a large number of provisions (loopholes) that greatly reduce the extent of graduation in practice. On this showing, there is at least public tolerance of a moderate amount of redistributive taxation.

However, we venture to suggest that the popularity of Reno, Las Vegas, and now Atlantic City is no less faithful an indication of the preferences of the public than the federal income tax, the editorials in the *New York Times* and the *Washington Post,* and the pages of the *New York Review of Books.*

Consequences of Egalitarian Policies

In shaping our own policy, we can learn from the experience of Western countries with which we share a common intellectual and cultural background and from which we derive many of our values. Perhaps the most instructive example is Great Britain, which led the way in the nineteenth century toward implementing equality of opportunity and in the twentieth toward implementing equality of outcome.

Since the end of World War II, British domestic policy has been dominated by the search for greater equality of outcome. Measure after measure has been adopted designed to take from the rich and give to the poor. Taxes were raised on income until they reached a top rate of 98 percent on property income and 83 percent on earned income and were supplemented by ever heavier taxes on inheritances. State-provided medical, housing, and other welfare services were greatly expanded, along with payments to the unemployed and the aged. Unfortunately, the results have been very different from those that were intended by the people who were quite properly offended by the class structure that dominated Britain for centuries. There has been a vast redistribution of wealth, but the end result is not an equitable distribution.

Instead, new classes of privileged have been created to replace or supplement the old: the bureaucrats, secure in their jobs, protected against inflation both when they work and when they retire; the trade unions that profess to represent the most downtrodden workers but in fact consist of the highest paid laborers in the land—the aristocrats of the labor movement; and the new millionaires—people who have been cleverest at finding ways around the laws, the rules, the regulations that have poured from Parliament and the bureaucracy, who have found ways to avoid paying taxes on their income and to get their wealth overseas beyond the grasp of the tax collectors. A vast reshuffling of income and wealth has taken place, greater equity, hardly.

The drive for equality in Britain failed, not because the wrong measures were adopted, though some no doubt were; not because they were badly administered, though some no doubt were; not because the wrong people administered them, though no doubt some did. The drive for equality failed for a much more fundamental reason. It went against one of the most basic instincts of all human beings. In the words of Adam Smith, that condition is "The uniform, constant, and uninterrupted effort of every man to better his condition"[9]—and, one may add, the condition of his children and his children's children. Smith, of course, meant by that condition not merely material well-being, though certainly that was one component. He had a much broader concept in mind, one that included all of the values by which men judge their success—in particular the kind of social values that gave rise to the outpouring of philanthropic activities in the nineteenth century.

When the law interferes with people's pursuit of their own values, they will try to find a way around. They will evade the law, they will break the law, or they will leave the country. Few of us believe in a moral code that justifies forcing people to give up much of what they produce to finance payments to persons they do not know for purposes they may not approve of. When the law contradicts what most people regard as moral and proper, they will break the law—whether the law is enacted in the name of a noble ideal such as equality or in the naked interest of one group at the expense of another. Only fear of punishment, not a sense of justice and morality, will lead people to obey the law.

When people start to break one set of laws, the lack of respect for the law inevitably spreads to all laws, even those that everyone regards as moral and proper—laws against violence, theft, and vandalism. Hard as it may be to believe, the growth of crude criminality in Britain in recent decades may well be one consequence of the drive for equality.

In addition, that drive for equality has driven out of Britain some of its ablest, best-trained, most vigorous citizens, much to the benefit of the United States and other countries that have given them a greater opportunity to use their talents for their own benefit. Finally, who can doubt the effect that the drive for equality has had on efficiency and productivity? Surely, that is one of the main reasons why economic growth in Britain has fallen so far behind its continental neighbors, the United States, Japan, and other nations over the past few decades.

We in the United States have not gone as far as Britain in promoting the goal of equality of outcome. Yet many of the same consequences are already evident—from a failure of egalitarian measures to achieve their objectives, to a reshuffling of wealth that by no standards can be regarded as equitable, to a rise in criminality, to a depressing effect on productivity and efficiency.

Capitalism and Equality

Everywhere in the world there are gross inequities of income and wealth. They offend most of us. Few can fail to be moved by the contrast between the luxury enjoyed by some and the grinding poverty suffered by others.

In the past century a myth has grown up that free market capitalism—equality of opportunity as we have interpreted that term—increases such inequalities, that it is a system under which the rich exploit the poor.

Nothing could be further from the truth. Wherever the free market has been permitted to operate, wherever anything approaching equality of opportunity has existed, the ordinary man has been able to attain levels of living never dreamed of before. Nowhere is the gap between rich and poor wider, nowhere are the rich richer and the poor poorer, than in those societies that do not permit the free market to operate. That is true of feudal societies like medieval Europe, India before independence, and much of modern South America, where inherited status determines position. It is equally true of centrally planned societies, like Russia or China or India since independence, where access to government determines position. It is true even where central planning was introduced, as in all three of these countries, in the name of equality.

Russia is a country of two nations: a small privileged upper class of bureaucrats, Communist Party officials, technicians, and a great mass of people living little better than their great-grandparents did. The upper class has access to special shops, schools, and luxuries of all kind; the masses are condemned to enjoy little more than the basic necessities. We remember asking a tourist guide in Moscow the cost of a large automobile that we saw and being told, "Oh, those aren't for sale; they're only for the Politburo." Several recent books by American journalists document in great detail the contrast between the privileged life of the upper classes and the poverty of the masses.[10] Even on a simpler level, it is noteworthy that the average wage of a foreman is a larger multiple of the average wage of an ordinary worker in a Russian factory than in a factory in the United States—and no doubt he deserves it. After all, an American foreman only has to worry about being fired; a Russian foreman also has to worry about being shot.

China, too, is a nation with wide differences in income—between the politically powerful and the rest; between city and countryside; between some workers in the cities and other workers. A perceptive student of China writes that "the inequality between rich and poor regions in China was more acute in 1957 than in any of the larger nations of the world except perhaps Brazil." He quotes another scholar as saying, "These examples suggest that the Chinese industrial wage structure is not significantly more egalitarian than that of other countries." And he concludes his examination of equality in China, "How evenly distributed would China's income be today? Certainly, it would not be as even as Taiwan's or South Korea's. . . . On the other hand, income distribution in China is obviously more even than in Brazil or South America. . . . We must conclude that China is far from being a society of complete equality. In fact, income differences in China may be quite a bit greater than in a number of countries commonly associated with 'fascist' elites and exploited masses."[11]

Industrial progress, mechanical improvement, and all the great wonders of the modern era have meant relatively little to the wealthy. The rich in Ancient Greece would have benefited hardly at all from modern plumbing: running servants replaced running water. Television and radio—the patricians of Rome could enjoy the leading musicians and actors in their home, could have the leading artists as domestic retainers. Ready-to-wear clothing, supermarkets; all these and many other modern developments would have added little to their life. They would have welcomed the improvements in transportation and in medicine, but for the rest, the great achievements of Western capitalism have redounded primarily to the benefit of the ordinary person. These achievements have made available to the masses conveniences and amenities that were previously the exclusive prerogative of the rich and powerful.

In 1848 John Stuart Mill wrote: "Hitherto it is questionable if all the mechanical inventions yet made have lightened the day's toil of any human being. They have enabled a greater population to live the same life of drudgery and imprisonment, and an increased number of manufacturers and others to make fortunes. They have increased the comforts of the middle classes. But they have not yet begun to effect those great changes in human destiny, which it is in their nature and in their futurity to accomplish."[12]

No one could say that today. You can travel from one end of the industrialized world to the other and almost the only people you will find engaging in backbreaking toil are people who are doing it for sport. To find people whose day's toil has not been lightened by mechanical invention, you must go to the non-capitalist world: to Russia, China, India, or Bangladesh, parts of Yugoslavia or to the more backward capitalist countries—to Africa, the Mideast, South America and, until recently, Spain or Italy.

Conclusion

A society that puts equality—in the sense of equality of outcome—ahead of freedom will end up with neither equality nor freedom. The use of force to achieve equality will destroy freedom, and the force, introduced for good purposes, will end up in the hands of people who use it to promote their own interests.

On the other hand, a society that puts freedom first will, as a happy by-product, end up with both greater freedom and greater equality. Though a by-product of freedom, greater equality is not an accident. A free society releases the energies and abilities of people to pursue their own objectives. It prevents some people from arbitrarily suppressing others. It does not prevent some people from achieving positions of privilege, but so long as freedom is maintained, it prevents those positions of privilege from becoming institutionalized; they are subject to continued attack by other able, ambitious people. Freedom means diversity but also mobility. It preserves the opportunity for today's disadvantaged to become tomorrow's privileged and, in the process, enables almost everyone, from top to bottom, to enjoy a fuller and richer life.

Notes

1. See J. R. Pole, *The Pursuit of Equality in American History* (Berkeley and Los Angeles: University of California Press, 1978), pp. 51–58.

2. Alexis de Tocqueville, *Democracy in America*, 2 vols., 2d ed., trans. Henry Reeve, ed. Francis Bowen (Boston: John Allyn, Publisher, 1863), vol. I, pp. 66–67. First French edition published in 1835.

3. Ibid., pp. 67–68.

4. See Smith, *The Russians*, and Kaiser, *Russia: The People and the Power*. Nick Eberstadt, "Has China Failed?" *New York Review of Books*, April 5, 1979, p. 37, notes, "In China, . . . income distribution seems *very roughly* to have been the same since 1953."

5. Helen Lefkowitz Horowitz, *Culture and the City* (Lexington: University Press of Kentucky, 1976), pp. ix–x.

6. Ibid., pp. 212 and 31.

7. "The Forgotten Man," in Albert G. Keller and Maurice R. Davis, eds., *Essays of William G. Sumner* (New Haven: Yale University Press, 1934), vol. I, pp. 466–96.

8. Robert Nozick, "Who Would Choose Socialism?" *Reason,* May 1978, pp. 22–23.

9. *Wealth of Nations,* vol. I, p. 325 (book II, chap. III).

10. See Smith, *The Russians,* and Kaiser, *Russia: The People and the Power.*

11. Nick Eberstadt, "China: How Much Success?" *New York Review of Books,* May 3, 1979, pp. 40–41.

12. John Stuart Mill, *The Principles of Political Economy* (1848), 9th ed. (London: Longmans, Green & Co., 1886), vol. II, p. 332 (Book IV, Chap. VI).

ELEVEN

THE MEANING OF FREEDOM

(1985)

This is a lecture series on the meaning and role of freedom. I thought it appropriate that in such a talk at West Point I should discuss the role of the military in a free society. That is a major issue and, for you young people, it is an important one in determining your future place in this great country.

One of the great achievements of the United States, a major pillar of our freedom has been the maintenance of civilian control of the military force. All of us tend to take the good things in our society for granted. We tend to worry about the bad things, but we take the good things for granted. And, because we do so, we seldom recognize how rare and unusual an achievement it is for a country to have a tradition in which civilian control is maintained over the military.

This special distinction of the United States goes back to the very founding of our country. After the end of the Revolutionary War, as I am sure many of you have been learning in your courses in American history, there was widespread dissatisfaction among the officers. The government of the United States, the Congress, acting under the Articles of Confederation, was disorganized. It had no money; we had been through an inflation; and the officers hadn't been paid.

One consequence of the widespread dissatisfaction was that a group of officers made a plan essentially for a military junta, a military takeover of the Congress. Some people who were later among our great national leaders, such as Alexander Hamilton, were part of the conspiracy. Their original idea was to persuade George Washington to head the coup d'etat. They also had in the background an alternate, namely, General Gates. They called a mass meeting at the headquarters of the American Army to discuss this issue. The mass meeting was to be attended by, and spoken to by, General Washington.

There is a marvelous four-volume biography of Washington by James Flexner. In my opinion, the most moving chapter in the whole four volumes is the chapter that describes what happened at this mass meeting. General Washington got up and, after making some initial comments opposing the whole idea that had little persuasive effect on the assembled officers, took from his pocket a folded piece of paper containing a letter that he wanted to read to the audience. He couldn't read it, so he reached in his other pocket to take out a pair of spectacles and said something about the fact that in the years of service he had given to his country, he had, unfortunately, been losing his eyesight. That scene moved those officers so much that it created an emotional situation in which there was a spontaneous rise of support for George Washington, who had come there to tell them that what they were planning was wrong, that the war had been fought to preserve freedom and independence, not to establish a new aristocracy or a new control by the military. There is no doubt that it was George Washington's behavior on that occasion to which this country owes the fact that the American Revolution ended differently than other revolutions.

Consider the other great revolutions. How did they end? The French Revolution ended ultimately with dictatorship by Napoleon. The Russian Revolution ended with dictatorship, first by Lenin and then by Stalin. The Chinese Revolution ended with a dictatorship by Mao. The emergence of independence in the countries in South America, in almost every single case, ended in dictatorship. The African countries, which in recent decades have achieved their independence, are almost all one-party countries with essentially a dictator in charge. It is hard to recall any other revolution in human history that has ended the way in which the American Revolution did, with a return to civilian control and without a takeover by a military or other dictator. And, as Flexner notes, we owe that to the personal characteristics of General George Washington of whom there is a magnificent statue I saw today in front of your buildings.

The experience of other countries, as well as this particular recent episode at home, was very much in the mind of the framers of the US Constitution. And you know, many of them objected to a standing army. Thomas Jefferson, when he became president, dissolved the standing army. He established West Point in order to train engineers, not soldiers. The framers of the Constitution provided (or did so subsequently in the Bill of Rights) for the right of citizens to bear arms. They wanted to depend on a voluntary militia, not on a standing army. So the fact that we have been able to maintain civilian control of the military for two hundred years is a remarkable achievement that we should recognize and not simply take for granted.

I want to talk about the question of principle that is involved in the relation between the military and the civilian economy as well as the question of practice. Why should there be a problem? Why does history show us that it is hard to reconcile military power, on the one hand, with human freedom, on the other. Reduced to its essentials, the answer, I believe, is very simple. It is because the basic principles of organization of military force and of a free society are the very opposite of one another.

There are only two fundamental ways that human activity can be organized that will enable large groups of people to cooperate toward some common objectives. One way is the method of command. That is the way of the army. The military is organized from the top down and it has to be organized that way. There is no alternative, given its particular purpose. We have seen it here tonight. The general gives the orders, and I march. The general gives the orders to the colonel, the colonel to the major, and so on, which is the fundamental principle of military organization, from the top down.

A free society, on the other hand, is the opposite. It's organized from the bottom up. The fundamental principle of a truly free society is voluntary cooperation among individuals who choose to cooperate with one another because all of them will benefit from doing so. I stated this to you in terms of the military versus a free society. In fact, the real conflict is more subtle. It is not so much between the military and civilians. It's fundamentally the difference between the use of political mechanisms to organize activity and the use of market mechanisms. It's political means versus market means.

When we choose to organize activity through political means, that inevitably involves command. It is true not only in the army but also elsewhere. The government is not financed by people voluntarily putting money into a hat. The government is financed by somebody commanding people to turn over so much money. The individual does not have a choice.

On the other hand, the miracle of the market (which is why the market is the essential foundation of a free society) is that it enables large numbers of people to cooperate together on a voluntary basis without anybody having to give any orders or commands. In the book called *Free to Choose,* based on the TV program, the general spoke about one of the books my wife and I have written together in which we used an example of a pencil. Two weeks ago we were in France, and we visited in the town of Grasse a perfume factory. It provided an equally interesting illustration of the miracle of the market. The perfume factory displayed a large chart with a map of the world showing where all the ingredients of the perfume came from. I don't remember the names of all exotic chemicals that were being used in order to make something that smelled nice on women. It's amazing the lengths to which people will go for that purpose. But, in any event, the chart showed items coming from the Fiji Islands, Indonesia, China, Hawaii, Oregon, and so on. Many of the items that were brought together in Grasse to be mixed chemically to make perfume were available only in the particular far-off places listed. Here literally thousands of people from all over the world were cooperating to produce perfume. They didn't speak the same language. They had different religions. Many of them hated one another, would have shot one another if they had met face-to-face. There was nobody sitting in a central office and sending out an order to the Fiji Islands to grow so much of this particular spice in order that it could be used in the perfume. And yet, somehow or other, these tens of thousands of people all over the world were cooperating together peacefully without anybody fighting, and it was all working.

The same thing is true if you contemplate the way the economy in general works. The organization of large-scale markets does not require a command economy. It can be done through voluntary cooperation and free markets. Indeed, all of the evidence suggests that the market mechanism is vastly superior to a command mechanism for organizing economic activity. As we have resorted more and more in the United States to political means, to trying to control a greater part of our society by political measures, we have increasingly threatened individual freedom because we have reduced the area within which voluntary cooperation operates and expanded the area in which command operates. In the process, we have also reduced our productivity.

I want to illustrate the problem more concretely for the military by using the example of the attitudes of the military to a volunteer force versus conscription. And I hope you will pardon me if I do so in part by telling a personal anecdote that happens to involve one of General Scott's predecessors. I was fortunate enough to be a member of President Nixon's Commission on an All-Volunteer Armed Force. I say fortunate because there are few things of which I am prouder than the role that I was able to play in ending conscription and bringing into being a volunteer armed force.

The commission had twelve members to begin with. At the outset, six of those members were in favor of a volunteer force, six were in favor of the continuation of conscription. (It was the so-called Gates Commission, headed by former secretary of defense Tom Gates.) At the end, we produced a unanimous report signed by all twelve people in favor of a volunteer armed force. One major dividend I got out of that experience personally was getting to know a great man, General Al Gruenther, who was a member of our commission.

At any rate, in the course of our work, we held hearings. One person who testified was General Westmoreland. He was then, I believe, chief of staff of the army, and he was testifying in that capacity. Like almost all military men who testified, he testified against a volunteer armed force. In the course of his testimony, he made the statement that he did not want to command an army of mercenaries. I stopped him and said, "General, would you rather command an army of slaves?" He drew himself back and said, "I don't like to hear our patriotic draftees referred to as slaves." I replied, "General, I don't like to hear our patriotic volunteers referred to as mercenaries." But I went on to say, "If they are mercenaries, then I, sir, am a mercenary professor, and you, sir, are a mercenary general; we are served by a mercenary physician, we use a mercenary lawyer, and we get our meat from a mercenary butcher." There is nothing wrong with a mercenary. That is the way the market operates. As Adam Smith said two hundred years ago, you do not owe your daily bread to the benevolence of your baker. You owe it to his desire to promote his own self-interest and to the fact that he finds that he can promote that self-interest in common with you.

I say this not in any way to criticize General Westmoreland. His attitude was typical of most people in the military. In one sense, that is a paradox. The officer corps in the military consists entirely of volunteers. Yet a large majority favor the use of conscription to fill the enlisted ranks. In another sense, it is entirely understandable. The military is formed on the basis of command. It seems natural to say that if you need soldiers, you should command them to be soldiers. And yet that is the very opposite of the basic principle on which this country is founded. This country is founded on the principle of free individuals who voluntarily contribute to the defense of their nation, who serve their nation because they believe in it and not because they'll go to jail if they don't. They serve because they believe in the cause for which the nation is fighting and because their fellow citizens are willing to reward them appropriately for performing that function. That's the question of principle, and it brings out very clearly the reason there has always been tension in a free society between the maintenance of a strong military force on the one side and the maintenance of human freedom, individual liberty, on the other.

So far as the question of practice is concerned, in the United States today, the principle of civilian control of the military is fortunately so firmly imbedded in our tradition that no one is seriously concerned about any threat to our political liberties from the military. That is the great achievement of the two hundred years of our tradition, but it does not mean that freedom in our society is safe. The major threat, in my opinion, comes from a very different source.

Freedom in our society is threatened not by the military but by the expansion of the role of government in our society. The threat is twofold. There is a direct threat because expanded government means less human freedom. There is an indirect threat, which is more directly relevant to this particular audience because the expansion of government tends to reduce the willingness of the public to maintain an adequate defense establishment.

From the beginning of our country, from say 1780 to 1930, spending by governments at all levels, federal, state, and local, never exceeded about 10 percent of the national income except during times of war, during the Civil War and the First World War. Spending by the federal government alone, the central government, never exceeded about 3 percent of the national income except, again, with the same exception of war. During each war, government spending shot up in order to pay for the cost of war. After the war, it came back down and settled again at 3 percent of the national income, half of which went to pay for the cost of military defense.

From the 1930s on, the scope and size of government expanded in a reaction to the Great Depression. Today government spending at all levels, federal, state, and local, amounts to over 40 percent of the national income. Federal spending alone is roughly about 30 percent of the national income, close to ten times as high as in 1930. In 1930 half of federal government spending was going for the military forces. Today, less than a quarter of federal government spending is going for the military.

You will again and again hear citizens around the country complain that the source of our budget deficit is excessive military spending. Maybe the spending is excessive, but that isn't the source of our deficit. That isn't where our major problem comes from. The situation is rather the reverse. The expansion of other forms of spending threatens the willingness of the people to support an adequate military force. Currently, every individual in the United States works from the first of January to sometime in June to pay for the expenses of government; only then can he start to work for himself. There would be nothing wrong with that if people were getting their money's worth. But hardly anyone thinks he's getting his money's worth.

Aside from getting your money's worth, the high government spending means that our freedom is reduced. To that extent we are not our own masters. We are working for somebody else. Over and above the effect of the spending of money on our freedom, there is an effect through restrictions and controls. There is no way in which anyone today can become a physician, a lawyer, a banker, a taxicab driver, in most states a beautician or a barber, without getting the permission of the government to do so. There is no way in which two people can make a mutually satisfactory arrangement to work together, for one to work for the other on terms that are mutually satisfactory, unless those terms conform to various government regulations. Ezra Stone's father and my mother could never have come to the United States at the age of fourteen if the United States had then had the laws and regulations that it has now. They would have been unable to be employed because they weren't worth what today the law requires you to pay any individual who is hired. So our freedom is threatened in many ways.

Nonetheless it is still true that this is the freest major country in the world. There is no comparison. Moreover, even more fortunately, a backlash is developing among the people in this country against the overextension of government. There is a widespread feeling that government has grown too large and needs to be cut back, that it's become too intrusive. I have a great deal of confidence that that change in opinion and attitudes of the people will be effective.

Let me return to the problem that is of more direct interest to this audience. The expansion of government has an indirect effect on our military strength. In the most recent book that my wife and I have published, called *Tyranny of the Status Quo,* we comment that the major threat to the national security of the United

States does not come from Russia. It comes from the growth of the welfare state. That seems like a silly, crazy statement. How can that be? The answer is simple. The expenditures that we are making on the welfare state absorb our taxable capacity and produce a great deal of pressure to cut down on what we spend on the military. When World War II started, total government spending in the United States was in the neighborhood of a quarter of the national income, with the federal government spending about half of that, about 12.5 percent of the national income. It was possible to increase that spending to 50 percent of the national income to fight the war. Today, when total government spending already absorbs as much as 40 percent of the national income and the federal government 30 percent, it would not be easy, indeed, not possible, to expand the amount on the military in case of a great emergency to anything like the same extent. Emergency aside, if you look at the political situation, it is hard to get funds for the military by raising taxes. People don't want to have their taxes raised. It is also hard to get funds by cutting programs that are already in effect. Each program has a small group that benefits very greatly from that program, and it will fight like the devil to avoid its being reduced. All of us will be willing to have military expenditures increased, provided it's done at somebody else's expense. When government spending is small and there is an urgent necessity to expand military spending, it is much easier to do at the expense of spending in general by raising taxes. When government spending is already very high, the situation is just the opposite. That is why nearly every politician favors cutting defense spending.

The freedom that we have enjoyed is a rare and precious achievement, and we shall not keep it unless we recognize the threats that beset it and act to offset it. And I believe the military has a very important role to play in this respect. The most obvious role is, of course, to maintain the tradition of civilian control of the military and to keep up the morale and effectiveness of the military force.

But I believe there is a much less obvious, but perhaps more important, role, which is for the military to make every effort to improve its operations so as to reduce the cost of providing for our military defense. The cost of providing for our national security is partly a question of foreign policy, of the commitments we undertake. That is not within the responsibilities of the military. Partly, however, the cost of the military forces is a question of the organization and the structure of the military itself. As you all know, there is very widespread criticism of the military for waste. Much attention is paid to the stories about screwdrivers that cost $1,000 and so on. Much of that criticism is not justified I am sure, but, unfortunately, much of it is justified. What are most clearly justified are the wasteful results of competition among the separate services. Each service has become a special interest, jealous of its own turf and unwilling to see it touched upon. There is a Joint Chiefs of Staff, but it is composed of people who have grown up within the separate services and whose loyalties are to the separate services. Just by calling the group Joint Chiefs of Staff, you don't make them joint. And so you have the very unpleasant spectacle, and one which does no good to the willingness of the American people to support adequate military forces, of each particular department of the military fighting against other departments to get its own project, rather than truly joining in a coordinated, cooperative venture for all.

I am not an expert on this subject, and I am not competent to judge how it can be solved. But I am sure that continued evidence of military waste, continued evidence of wasteful competition among the services, will even further erode the willingness of the populace to support the military forces we need to defend this nation against foreign enemies. I am also sure that if we are going to succeed in maintaining adequate military forces, two things will have to happen. I and my fellow citizens will have to be successful in checking the growth of government spending in general, and you and your fellow members of the armed services will have to devote more attention and more care than you have so far devoted to making sure that the American taxpayer gets more for his money in the way of national defense. This is a great country, and we can keep it great. But it will not stay a great country unless we continue to fight, and to work, and to strive to make it one. Thank you.

TWELVE

FREE MARKETS AND FREE SPEECH

(1987)

I am not accustomed to speaking to lawyers or putative lawyers, but we do have at least one thing in common. Economics and law are, I understand, almost the only two professions that have the characteristic that the supply creates its own demand.

I was told that my function is to put the symposium about the First Amendment in a broader context. I shall try to do that by considering two major issues: first, how free speech, press, and assembly fit into the broader context of a free society and, second, the case for a free society. The label I like to use to refer to the views I shall express is liberalism, by which I mean real honest-to-God liberalism, not the fake version that goes by that name these days. I mean nineteenth-century liberalism. These days, nineteenth-century liberals have felt compelled to refer to themselves as libertarians or conservatives, even when those names are thoroughly inappropriate. Professor Schumpeter put it best when he wrote, "[a]s a supreme, if unintended, compliment, the enemies of the system of private enterprise have thought it wise to appropriate its label."[1]

Let me start by asking a question that I discussed a number of years ago: Do free men make free markets, or do free markets make free men? That sounds like a play on words, like a purely semantic question, but it is not at all. There is some connection both ways. But there is little doubt in my mind that the connection from free markets to free men is much stronger than the connection from free men to free markets. The framers of our Constitution, the founders of our country—George Washington, James Madison, Thomas Jefferson, Alexander Hamilton—were free men, and as free men they made a society that developed as a free society. But if you had asked Lenin and Trotsky, you would have found that they too regarded themselves as free men; but by no means did they make a free society. Much more important, intellectuals generally regard themselves as free men and invariably favor freedom for themselves. Many—perhaps most—of them, however, favor introducing collectivism into society in every other area. Alexander Hamilton is a good example. His *Report on Manufactures* gave lip service throughout to Adam Smith, yet the report was really devoted to undermining a basic component of a free society, namely, free trade.[2] It favored the enactment of tariffs and other restrictions on trade. It fostered a step toward collectivism. Although Hamilton was certainly a free man, in *Report on Manufactures* he was not working for a free society. That has generally been true of most intellectuals.

Free societies have emerged in considerable part as a result of accident, not of intellectual ideas. Though intellectual ideas have played an important role, it is hard to regard them as the prime movers. For example, something that had nothing to do with ideas was a major factor enabling the United States society to be as free as it has been: the panic of 1837. Those of you who have studied American history know that in the 1820s and 1830s there was a great outburst of governmental involvement in industrial, manufacturing, and other enterprises. Many states built and operated canals. Illinois, Indiana, and other states set up government banking systems. No ideological objections prevented widespread intervention by government—primarily state rather than federal—into economic activity and economic projects. Fortunately (in retrospect, though the people did not like it at the time), there was a great financial panic in 1837 in which most government enterprises went bust. That gave state socialism, to give it its modern label, a bad name and, in my opinion, had a major impact on the future development of the United States. I believe that it had more to do with the government staying out of business than did the laissez-faire philosophy represented by *The Wealth of Nations,* even though *The Wealth of Nations* provided the intellectual justification for the course that the United States largely followed.[3]

This seems to be true in Great Britain, where the philosophy developed and where Adam Smith wrote *The Wealth of Nations* in 1776. It took seventy years before the so-called corn laws were repealed[4] (as you know, corn referred to all manner of grain). The campaign for eliminating tariffs on corn, which persisted for decades and ultimately led to the repeal of the corn laws, had as its major theme the idea that a group of grasping, selfish landowners were exploiting the ordinary people. The repeal of the tariffs on corn established free trade as a basic principle of British economic policy. Without restrictions on international trade, it is extremely difficult to prevent free competition at home. Indeed, freedom of competition in international trade is the most important single measure that can be taken to promote and preserve a free market economy.

It is no accident that, in the twentieth century, Britain reimposed tariffs and other restrictions on trade as it moved away from a primarily private-enterprise economy toward a socialist, collectivist economy. Such restrictions were an early component of what has become the modern welfare state.

There is a direct connection between free markets on the one hand and free speech on the other. That is part of the story of free markets making free men. Interferences with markets constitute and produce interferences with free speech. Let me give some specific examples.

Compare the tycoons of the nineteenth century in the United States with the tycoons of today. With few exceptions, today's tycoons are not very colorful; they wear three-button suits and go to Washington to get the best deal they can from the government. They rarely speak out against any government program. The tycoons of the nineteenth century, when government played a much smaller role, when spending by the federal government amounted to 3 percent of the national income instead of the 30 percent it does now, were much more outspoken. They were characters, and they did not hesitate to express themselves.

No major businessman today in our country has freedom of speech. He would not dare to speak freely. Let me illustrate with a couple of recent quotations from the *Wall Street Journal*. The first is from an editorial of February 26, 1986.

> It is not clear that any federal regulatory agency has more power to intimidate the people it regulates than the Food and Drug Administration. As a consequence few active medical researchers in the United States will publicly criticize the FDA bureaucracy. Earlier this week a small California pharmaceutical company was the latest to learn how high the cost can be for having the temerity to take public issue with this agency.[5]

The next day, in a discussion of small artificial hearts intended to be used for women and an FDA ruling prohibiting their use (incidentally, a clear case of sex discrimination): "'It's crazy and bizarre that we've gotten into this circumstance with this regulatory agency making medical decisions,' said one of the heart surgeons, adding, 'I don't know if I want to be quoted on that because I have to live with those guys.'"[6]

A few years ago, after the Arab cartel was established and the price of oil shot up, the government both enforced price controls on oil and introduced a complex system of allocations and entitlements involving extensive government regulation of the oil industry. I received at that time a letter from an executive vice president of an oil and gas association, who, needless to say, did not want his name used publicly. He wrote: "As you know, the real issue more so than the price per cubic foot is the continuation of the First Amendment to the Constitution. With increasing regulation, as Big Brother looks closer over our shoulders, we grow timid about speaking out for truths and our beliefs against falsehoods and wrongdoings. Fear of IRS audits, bureaucratic strangulation, and government harassment is a powerful weapon against freedom of speech."

Another one of my favorite examples of what I regard as an extraordinary infringement on freedom of speech has to do with the selling of United States savings bonds. The situation is not so bad today as it was about five or ten years ago, when inflation was sharply on the rise and when anyone who bought a United States savings bond was certain to end up after twenty-five years with less purchasing power than he had given up in buying it; I used to call the promotion of United States savings bonds the biggest bucket-shop operation in American history. Yet almost every bank in the United States included in one or more of its monthly statements a brochure urging the depositors to buy United States savings bonds to benefit themselves and to promote the country's welfare.

Moreover, both then and now, a full-page advertisement by a committee of businessmen appears each year in all the major newspapers of the country, an advertisement that contains pictures of the president of this company and the president of that company and that urges people to buy United States savings bonds. Some time ago, I asked a lot of bank presidents and other persons on the businessmen's committee, "Would you advise a customer or friend of yours to put any of his money in US savings bonds?" They invariably answered, "Of course not, it's a terrible investment." "Why then," I asked, "do you send out the misleading advertising that's provided to you by the Treasury Department? Why do you serve on the committee?" The answer was always the same: "The Treasury and the Federal Reserve wouldn't like it if I didn't."

Do those gentlemen have freedom of speech? Did any of those bankers have freedom of speech? You may say, "They just didn't have any guts. They could have made speeches about the fraud that was being perpetrated upon the American public in asking them to buy savings bonds paying interest rates of 4 or 5 percent when inflation was at the rate of 8 or 9 percent." And perhaps some did. Making such a speech, however, would have imposed a very heavy cost. There is nothing wrong in there being some cost in engaging in free speech—there is no free lunch, and there is no free free speech. But the cost ought to be reasonable, not excessive. And it is excessive.

"Well," you may say, "what is disturbing about such restraints? They affect businessmen only, and it doesn't matter whether businessmen have free speech." That may not be your attitude, but I assure you it would be the attitude of those in many places, including many—perhaps most—faculty clubs and common rooms of universities. The restraints on freedom of speech are not limited to business. Look at academics. Consider medical people, engaging in research funded by grants from the National Institutes of Health. I am sure that some among them privately question whether that is an appropriate way to spend the taxpayers' money. But how many members of a medical school faculty, even those who have received no research grants, would regard it as consistent with their future professional career to come out publicly against government subsidization of research in medicine?

In my own field of economics it was proposed some years ago that the National Science Foundation cease giving grants in economics or at least reduce drastically the amount granted. Many of my professional colleagues in various universities issued a public letter strenuously objecting to any proposal to eliminate or reduce such grants for economic research. I wrote a column in *Newsweek*[7] in the form of an open letter in which I urged the abolition of the National Science Foundation altogether. I cannot say that I was popular with my fellow economists. But why was I able to express such a view at all and do so without any concern about adverse consequences? Because at the time I was a tenured professor approaching retirement. About the only people in this country today who have effective freedom of speech are tenured professors approaching retirement.

So you can see that there is a close relationship between freedom in the marketplace and freedom in other areas and that, moreover, freedom in the marketplace produces freedom elsewhere. In the marketplace transactions are fundamentally anonymous. People are cooperating with one another because both sides benefit. In the marketplace, individuals do not have the power to coerce other individuals. Anyone who refuses to do business with another because he does not like his opinions on an unrelated matter hurts himself, and primarily himself, in the process. Those are the reasons that a free marketplace is such an important element in a free society.

Rose and I entitled the final chapter of our book *Free to Choose*[8] "The Tide Is Turning." The tide, with respect to ideas, has continued to turn. There is much support today for views that were regarded as beyond the pale twenty to twenty-five years ago. Those of us who were a small, beleaguered minority some thirty or thirty-five years ago no longer are in the minority.

If you look, however, not at ideas but at practice, at the nature of the world and of the United States in particular, the tide has not turned. On the contrary, the United States today is a less free society than it was thirty years ago. Government has expanded in every dimension. Government spending has gone up as a fraction of income; government taxes have gone up as a fraction of income; regulatory agencies of every kind have proliferated. Fewer people today have effective freedom of speech. Though, as intellectuals, we may emphasize freedom of speech, to the majority of people in the United States the freedom to buy what they want to buy, the freedom to live where they want to live, and the freedom to be employed as they want to be employed are at least as important as the intellectual freedom that is so important to us.

In those aspects of society, people today are less free than they were thirty or forty years ago. Indeed, this cumulative movement toward a less free society has, in my opinion, been a major reason that the tide has been turning in the intellectual area. The growth of the United States government has made its defects more apparent, as have the failures of collectivism in Russia and in every other country where it has been tried. Those events have caused a change in ideas. But that change in ideas has not yet been translated into a change in the world of practice. That battle must still be fought.

I want to turn to a very different topic. So far, I have been taking it for granted that a free society is the right kind of society, that it is the kind of society we want or ought to want. There is an obligation to try to spell out the basis for that belief. Obviously, that is a subject of immense depth, subtlety, and profundity that is beyond my competence. A few comments, however, may not be inappropriate.

A free society, I believe, is a more productive society than any other; it releases the energies of people, enables resources to be used more effectively, and enables people to have a better life.

But that is not why I am in favor of a free society. I believe and hope that I would favor a free society even if it were less productive than some alternative, say, a slave society. It is fortunate that that is not the case because the only reason that there is a ghost of a chance of having something approximating a free society is that a free society is so productive. The enemies of a free society, the forces that are working against it, are so strong that the major thing, in my opinion, that prevents them from conquering is that a free society is so productive that it tends to overwhelm those other forces if given half a chance.

I favor a free society because my basic value is freedom itself. I define freedom as the absence of coercion of one person by another. To define it in a positive way, it is the freedom of individuals to engage in voluntary cooperation one with another so long as they do not affect third parties. The question is this: How do I justify that preference? How can I justify saying that people ought to be allowed to go their own way and not be interfered with by others? How can I justify letting people be free to sin? If I really knew what sin is, I could not justify it. All totalitarians, all people who have suppressed freedom, have done so because of the arrogance of their believing that they knew what sin was. The ayatollah knows what sin is, which is why women in Iran must not walk around without having their faces covered. He cannot let them be free to do otherwise because he is firmly convinced that he knows what sin is. He is the archetype of a "true believer."

One justification for letting people be free to sin is that there is no merit in people's not sinning if they are prevented from sinning by coercion. There is merit in not sinning only if people do not sin because of their own volition. I believe, however, that that is not a satisfactory answer if you really know what sin is.

In my opinion, the real case for a free society and for freedom is ignorance—we cannot be sure we are right. If I cannot persuade people by reason and argument and talk, if I cannot persuade them to agree with me, what right do I have to force them? How can I be sure that I am right? I have always been fond of a quotation that is attributed to Cromwell but that of course he meant for the benefit of others, not himself. He said, "I beseech you, in the bowels of Christ, think it possible you may be mistaken."[9] I think that states the essence of the case for a free society.

In short, the basic virtue in a free society and the basic justification for a free society is humility, a willingness to recognize that no matter how strongly one may believe he is correct, he cannot be sure. Hence he does not have the right to force his view on someone else.

In conclusion, I want to give two examples to illustrate the relation between the different aspects of freedom that I have been talking about. Some years ago I received from an academic at a university in Pakistan a letter that read as follows: "I have been delving into the political philosophy of liberalism and individualism and have read whatever little on the subject is available in our libraries. It has been my great misfortune that your highly popular work, *Capitalism and Freedom,*[10] is not present in the libraries of this country. Exchange control regulations in this country prevent me from buying it from a publisher in the United States." Now I ask you, was that a restriction of his economic freedom? Of his political freedom? Of his intellectual freedom? Can you logically make a distinction? Is our United States system of tariff protection a restriction of our economic freedom or of our intellectual freedom or of our political freedom? I think it is clearly a restriction of all.

My second example is a hypothetical example, not a real one. Every tobacco company in this country is required to put a warning label on cigarettes that states that smoking cigarettes may be harmful to your health. It is taken for granted by almost everybody that requiring such a warning label is not a violation of free speech. There is, however, little doubt in my mind, and I am sure most of you will agree with me, that far more lives have been lost in the past century as a result of Karl Marx's *Das Kapital*[11] than from smoking cigarettes. Would it therefore be appropriate to require every copy of *Das Kapital* to carry a warning label reading, "This book may be dangerous to social and personal health?" Where is the difference? Yet is there any doubt that there would be a great outcry at that suggestion? Such a requirement would be regarded—and, I may say, rightly so—as clearly an interference with the right of people to read what they want to read and so on. I challenge you to find any significant difference. Needless to say, I am not a defender of cigarettes. I quit smoking some twenty-odd years ago because I was persuaded by the evidence I read. But I quit because I was persuaded; I do not think it is any business of the rest of you to tell me whether I ought to have quit or not.

Finally, let me summarize everything I have been saying by saying that for an effectively free society we need the First Amendment that we have but we need a parallel amendment at least as much. And that parallel amendment should read as follows: Congress shall make no laws forbidding voluntary acts between consenting adults.

Notes

1. J. Schumpeter, *History of Economic Analysis* 394 (1954).

2. A. Hamilton, *Report on Manufactures* (Philadelphia, 1791).

3. A. Smith, *An Inquiry into the Nature and Causes of the Wealth of Nations* (London, 1776).

4. *See* 9 and 10 Vict., ch. 25 (1846) (reducing but not completely abolishing the duties on grain). All duties on grain ceased in 1869. *See* 32 and 33 Vict., ch. 14, § 4 (1869).

5. *Wall Street Journal,* Feb. 26, 1986, at 24, col. 1.

6. *Wall Street Journal,* Feb. 27, 1986, at 24, col. 3.

7. Friedman, "Open Letter on Grants," *Newsweek,* May 18, 1981, at 99.

8. M. Friedman and R. Friedman, *Free to Choose* (1980).

9. Letter to the General Assembly of the Church of Scotland (Aug. 3, 1650), reprinted in J. Bartlett, *Familiar Quotations* 272 (15th ed., 1980).

10. M. Friedman, *Capitalism and Freedom* (1962).

11. K. Marx, *Das Kapital* (Berlin, 1867).

THIRTEEN

WHERE ARE WE
ON THE ROAD TO LIBERTY?

(1987)

In the past few decades there has been a sea change in the direction of the ideas of the public. The climate of opinion has moved sharply toward belief in a greater role for free markets and belief that big government is the problem and not the solution.

On the other hand, in the world of practice—the world in which we live—we are now farther from a free society than we were thirty or forty years ago. The world of ideas has gone one way, and up to now the world of practice has gone the other way. And those two movements, though superficially contradictory, are closely connected. In my opinion, the major reason that we have made progress in the world of ideas is precisely because we have regressed in the world of practice.

Consider first the world of ideas. I recently wrote a new preface for a reissue of my wife's and my book, *Capitalism and Freedom*, originally published in 1962. Referring to the time when the lectures incorporated in the book were given, I wrote: "It is hard even for persons who were then active, let alone for the more than half of the current population who were then less than ten years old or had not yet been born, to reconstruct the intellectual climate of the times. Those of us who were deeply concerned about the danger to freedom and prosperity from the growth of government, from the triumph of welfare state and Keynesian ideas, were a small beleaguered minority regarded as eccentrics by the great majority of our fellow intellectuals."

One bit of evidence in support of that description of the intellectual climate at the time is the treatment that our book received. Here was a book directed at the general public that was destined to sell more than 400,000 copies in the next eighteen years, written by an established professor at a leading university and published by a leading university press. Yet it was not reviewed in a single popular American publication. It was not reviewed in the *New York Times,* the *New York Herald Tribune* (which was in existence then), or even the *Chicago Tribune* or in *Time* or *Newsweek.* It *was* reviewed by the London *Economist* and by the major professional journals. But it is inconceivable that a book of the same kind on the other side of the subject by an economist of comparable professional standing would have received a similar silent treatment.

By contrast, as evidence of the change in the intellectual climate of opinion, consider the very different reception of the book my wife and I published in 1980, *Free to Choose,* which was reviewed by every major publication. As further evidence, consider the comments Heritage president Ed Fuelner recently made at a dinner there. He drew a sharp contrast between the few and sparse think tanks on our side some three decades ago and the number now. He could mention only four that existed back then: the Hoover Institution, which is still here today; ISI, at that time called the Intercollegiate Society of Individualists, which has changed its name but kept the initials; an embryonic AEI (American Enterprise Institute), as he described it; and CSIS (Center for Strategic and International Studies). He should also have included Leonard Read's Foundation for Economic Education (FEE), which really originated in Los Angeles with Leonard's work at the Los Angeles Chamber of Commerce.

By contrast Ed reeled off a long list of additional institutions currently devoted to developing and spreading the idea of limited government and free markets, plus a host of others trying to translate ideas into action. Similarly with respect to publications, the only one he could think of that was devoted to promoting the ideas of freedom thirty to forty years ago was FEE's *Freeman.* Today, we can list a whole series of publications on that general side, though with great differences in specific areas—*National Review, Human Events, American Spectator, Policy Review,* and *Reason.* But I belabor the obvious in stressing how great has been the change in the intellectual climate of opinion.

The more interesting question is, why has there been so great a shift in the attitudes of the public? I'm sorry to confess that I do not believe it occurred because of the persuasive power of such books as Friedrich Hayek's *Road to Serfdom* or Ayn Rand's *Fountainhead* or *Atlas Shrugged* or our own *Capitalism and Freedom.* Such books certainly played a role, but I believe the major reason for the change is the extraordinary force of factual evidence— and that is the link between the world of ideas and the world of practice.

The great hopes that had been placed in Russia and China by the collectivists and socialists turned into ashes. It is very hard today for the pilgrims who seek the new future to find much sustenance in places like Russia and China; indeed, the only hope in those countries comes from China's recent moves toward the free market. The pilgrims today are driven to going to Nicaragua and Cuba. Similarly, the hopes that were placed in Fabian socialism and the welfare state in Britain or the New Deal in the United States were disappointed. One major government program after another started with the very best aims and with noble objectives and turned out not to deliver the goods.

Hardly anyone today anywhere in the world will say that the way to get efficient production is through nationalized enterprises or that the way to solve every social problem is to have government throw more money at them. In that area we have won the battle. The left is intellectually bankrupt. The neoconservatives are correct in defining themselves as (modern) liberals mugged by reality—still retaining many of their earlier values but driven to recognize that they cannot achieve them through government. They are somewhat reluctant libertarians, at least on economic issues, but largely libertarians nonetheless.

In this country, the Vietnam War helped undermine belief in the beneficence of government. And most of all, as the great British constitutional lawyer, A. V. Dicey, predicted nearly seventy-five years ago, the rising burden of taxation produced a reaction from the general public against the growth of government and the spread of its influence.

Ideas played their part. But they played their part not by producing a reaction against the spread of government but by determining the form that that reaction took. The role we play as intellectuals is not to persuade anybody but to keep options open and to provide alternative policies that can be adopted when people decide they have to make a change.

What about the world of practice? We are farther from our ideal of a free society than we were thirty to forty years ago in almost every dimension. Take the most obvious: in 1950 spending by federal, state, and local governments was 25 percent of national income; in 1985 it was 44 percent. And in order to get a real basis of comparison, in 1930 it was 15 percent. Everybody in the country is working today until nearly the middle of June to pay for the expenses of government before they can start paying for their own expenses. It was bad enough thirty-five years ago when people were working until after April Fools' Day.

In the past thirty years, a host of new government agencies have been created. We now have a Department of Energy, a Department of Education, a National Endowment for the Arts and another for the Humanities, Environmental Protection Agency, Occupational and Health and Safety Organization, and on and on. We have a whole sequence of additional agencies whereby civil servants decide for us what is in our best interest. In *Capitalism and Freedom* we listed fourteen "activities currently undertaken by government in the US that cannot . . . validly be justified in terms of the principles" of a liberal society. This list is far from comprehensive. And only one of those activities—military conscription—has been terminated.

A couple of others have shown some slight improvement; airlines have been deregulated, and regulation Q, which limited the interest rates that banks could pay on deposits, was eliminated. But most activities have been made more extensive, and many new ones have been added.

Contrasting 1985 with 1950 is unduly pessimistic in some ways because there *has* been a change: ideas have started to have an influence. But the most you can say is that the rate of expansion of government spending has been slowed down, not reversed. Government spending as a fraction of income has continued to go up; only the *rate* of increase has slown down. We're going to hell a little more slowly, but we're still going in that direction.

There have been a few victories. We did, after all, get rid of the Civil Aeronautics Board that regulated the airlines. We did get rid of military conscription—that's something truly to celebrate. But the improvement has been meager. The most one can say is that no major new spending programs have been passed in the last six years. The increase in government spending, outside the military, has been predominantly the effect of earlier programs. So we can be a bit more optimistic by narrowing our focus and looking at the last five or six years.

I do not cite the contrast between the world of ideas and the world of practice as a reason for either dismay or pessimism; on the contrary, it reflects a typical situation. There always is and always has been a long lag between a change in the climate of opinion and a change in actual policy. Let me cite Dicey again. In his great book *Law and Public Opinion in the Nineteenth Century,* he wrote: "The opinion which changes the law is in one sense the opinion of the time when the law is actually altered; in another sense it has often been in England the opinion prevalent some twenty or thirty years before that time; it has been as often as not in reality the opinion not of the day but of yesterday." History suggests that trends in practice lag long after trends in opinion.

Take the situation in 1776, the year in which Adam Smith published *The Wealth of Nations,* with its case for free trade—and also, interestingly, the year of the Declaration of Independence in this country. It was seventy years before the Corn Laws were abolished in Britain and free trade was achieved. Yet Adam Smith started to win the battle in the world of ideas in the eighteenth century. The belief in laissez-faire and free markets lasted for seventy-five to a hundred years, until the 1870s or so. Policy followed, but it didn't really start rolling until early in the nineteen century. And it continued rolling in the same direction after a new trend started in the world of ideas—a trend away from free markets and laissez-faire and toward Fabian socialism and the welfare state.

That trend of opinion also lasted for nearly a hundred years, into the 1950s or '60s, but it too influenced policy only after a long lag. In Britain the change in policies did not occur until just before World War I, say 1908–14. In the United States the change did not occur until the New Deal in 1933. The same thing is happening now. Ideas, the climate of opinion, started to change in the 1940s or '50s—slowly at first. The trend of opinion has been gathering strength, and it will continue to do so. But policy has been lagging behind and has only recently started to move in the same direction.

The real lesson to be drawn from this contrast between what has been happening in the world of ideas and what has been happening in the world of practice is that we cannot afford to relax our efforts and coast in the belief that the job is done. On the contrary, the truly hard job lies ahead. Of course we want agreement with our ideas—but primarily as a step toward the translation of those ideas into practice. We want to promote an expansion of the freedom of individuals to use their resources in accordance with their own values.

Although we are no longer an isolated remnant or simply a kooky group of people, we are still fighting against the odds. And the odds include most of us as well. We must not kid ourselves; we must not suppose that we are different from the rest of our fellow citizens. I include in the odds that we are facing all the businessmen who are in favor of freedom for everyone else, provided they can get special taxes or a tariff or regulatory treatment for themselves. We have to face the problem of the intellectuals, our colleagues at the universities and academies, who are in favor of freedom for themselves provided they can control everybody else.

More important, we are battling the economic inertia that derives from the interest every one of us has in retaining any privilege or benefit he has been able to accumulate and has come to regard as his right. Each of us is capable of truly believing that what is good for us is good for the country and thereby justifying a special exception to the general rule we profess to favor. Over and over I am impressed by the letters I receive from people who say, "Oh, I agree with you thoroughly, I agree with your views, but"; and it's that "but." The most extreme case I had recently was somebody who agreed fully with me about free trade but thought the bee industry was an exception. His excuse was the importance of having bees to pollinate fruit trees and other plants.

So it would be a mistake to suppose that because we have largely won the intellectual battle, because the left is intellectually bankrupt, we have also won the practical battle, the battle of changing the policy of the country and moving in the right direction. We are very far from that. Certainly most of us, including myself, are disappointed in how little we have managed to accomplish in the past six years under circumstances that could not have been more favorable. We have had a president who, though you may disagree with some of his particular positions, is clearly committed to reducing the size and scope and role of government and who has been willing to stick to his principles—the first president in my lifetime (and I suspect in yours) who was elected not because he said what the people wanted to hear but because the people had come to want to hear what he had been saying for a long time.

And yet in the period of his ascendancy the most we have succeeded in doing is preventing the growth of government from increasing still more. In some areas we have moved forward, but we certainly have not achieved as much as most of us had hoped.

But this is not a reason for distress. It is in line with what history tells us: these movements do not come easily and overnight, but once you get started in a certain direction you tend to keep on going that way. The prospect is bright but only if we continue trying to spread our ideas and persuade *ourselves,* more important than anyone else, to be consistent with the beliefs we profess.

FOURTEEN

THE FOUNDATIONS
OF A FREE SOCIETY

(1988)

Herbert Giersch's reference, in his splendidly comprehensive talk, to the first meeting of the Mont Pèlerin Society developed in me an irrepressible urge to introduce a few comments, before the remarks I had intended to make, about the contrast between the situation as we saw it on top of that mountain in Switzerland and the situation as it is today. In drawing that comparison I am less optimistic about what has happened between then and now than Herbert is. What is true and clear is that the problem those of us who are determined to defend a free society face is very different now than it was in 1947. As we met there in Mont Pèlerin, the place that gave the name to our society because we couldn't agree on any other—disagreement is a long tradition in the Mont Pèlerin Society, I'm glad to say, and I'm delighted to see that it continues to flourish—the problem that we regarded as preeminent was how to avoid comprehensive central planning. That was the danger that we thought would undermine freedom. Our countries had come out of war, whether on the defeated side or on the victorious side, with a great panoply of central control of the major resources of society. There was widespread intellectual belief that central control was inevitable and necessary for an efficient use of human and natural resources. With respect to that problem, we can say it no longer exists. It would be hard to find anywhere in the world today someone who would say that the road to prosperity is through detailed, comprehensive central control and direction of economic resources. Surely there are no such people in either Russia or China, let alone in Britain, the United States, or Germany.

However, another problem emerged. If the state was not to be used for comprehensive central planning, that did not prevent a drive to use the state for something else. That something else quickly turned to be how to use the state to take money from some and give it to others. Redistribution of income and wealth turned out to be the overwhelming problem and agenda of the next forty-odd years. Herbert said, and correctly, that our ideas have been victorious. They have in a sense. They have in the area of belief, in the area of intellectual climate. The spread of the notion of greater use of market forces is a tribute to those ideas. However, suppose you ask yourself a different question: Are governments weaker today or stronger, not in ideas, not in their hold upon people's intellectual allegiance, but in practice, than they were in 1947? The answer is abundantly clear. I doubt that there is a country in the then free world or today's free world in which government spending as a fraction of income is not higher today than it was forty years ago. In that area we have lost the battle, not won it. We still have the battle to win. We tend to look at things from the point of view of the immediate past. There is an inevitable tendency to regard what is as somehow the appropriate base, the appropriate starting point, but that way lies defeat.

We have, and now I am getting into the substance of what I intended to say, a lot of talk—Herbert contributed some of it— saying that we have a more open society today than we did in the immediate postwar period. In one respect we do. There is no doubt whatsoever that advances in computers, in communication, in satellites have made the world more open to information and that securities trading is more open and can be conducted on a twenty-four-hour-a-day basis around the world. But are we more open in other respects? Is our trade more open in people and in goods? Very doubtful.

If we really want to get a picture of what openness means, what are the foundations of a truly free and open society, I suggest that we will do well by looking back to a much earlier date. Let me quote two statements about the way the world was some seventy-five years ago, when it was far more open than it is today. The first is a quote from John Maynard Keynes, from his 1919 book on *The Economic Consequences of the Peace.* Before August 1914, "the inhabitants of London . . . could secure forthwith, if he wished it, cheap and comfortable means of transit to any country or climate without passport or other formality, . . . could then proceed abroad to foreign quarters, without knowledge of their religion, language or customs, bearing coined wealth upon his person, and would consider himself greatly aggrieved and surprised at the least interference." Let me give you another quote, this one from the late Bertram Wolfe, a longtime fellow at the Hoover Institution who Glenn was so eloquent about and who served with Glenn. In his autobiography, he wrote:

> How remote now seems that world into which I was born, in which one could buy a ticket to anywhere on the face of the earth—except Turkey or Russia—without presenting an identity card, a passport, or a visa. . . . Up to 1914 a passport was a luxury, a privilege of the envoy or of the wealthy traveler, in which his government introduced him and commended him to the hospitality of foreign officials, never a necessity for the humbler citizen or the refugee seeking some spot on the planet where he might come to rest and resume his full status as a human being.

> My existence in my young manhood was attested to by my mere
> physical presence, without documents, forms, permits, licenses,
> orders, lists of currency carried in and out, identity cards, draft
> cards, ration cards, exit stamps, customs declarations, question-
> naires, tax forms, reports in multiple, or authentications of my birth,
> being, nationality, status, beliefs, color, creed, right to be, enter,
> leave, move about, work, trade, purchase, dwell.[1]

Now those are descriptions of a truly open society, and they are
very, very far indeed from where we are today.

What are the basic components of a truly open society? I believe
we can classify the basic components of a truly free and open society under three headings: first, individual freedom—free speech,
free press, free assembly, freedom of religion. Even in those countries today in which those freedoms are greatest, they are very
far from being what they were a hundred years ago. Consider my
own country, the United States, which prides itself on its freedom
and rightly so. Among at least the large countries, it is the freest
country in the world. Yet a world in which government distrib-
utes well over 40 percent of the national income is not a world in
which people speak freely. How many heads of corporations, let
alone how many professors in universities, really feel free to come
out and criticize governmental arrangements that provide their
daily bread? Some courageous people are willing to take chances,
but in the main we are very far from having truly free speech. Just
look at the advertisements that used to be put out, signed by the
heads of all the major banks in the country, telling people to buy
US savings bonds. Every person who signed that advertisement
knew that the savings bond was a bad deal, that when it matured
would buy less than the money paid for it would have had at the
time of purchase. I asked many of them, "Why did you sign that
advertisement?" They all told me the same thing: "The Federal
Reserve wouldn't like it if we didn't." So individual freedom is

more than statements in the Bill of Rights that you are free, that Congress shall make no laws interfering with freedom of speech or religion. That is certainly important and desirable, but it is more than that, which cannot be maintained effectively in a society in which government controls a very large fraction of total resources.

The second major component is a rule of law, a relatively stable, well-defined, impersonal body of rules that people can count on, interpreted by an independent judiciary. That is to be contrasted with rule by people, arbitrary control of some people by others. We speak of the rule of law rather than the rule of men. Again, in principle, we have the rule of law in our free societies. But do we in the same sense in which we had it a hundred years ago? I do not believe so. I speak again of the United States because that's what I'm most familiar with. Does anyone who faces an Internal Revenue agent believe he is being ruled by impersonal law? Hardly. Does he when he applies for a license from a governmental bureau that can be judge, jury, and executioner? And so on down the line. So here again we have a great deal to achieve.

The third essential component is the market economy, which itself in my opinion can be expressed as a trinity. (Everything comes in three parts. There was once an article in the *Journal of the American Statistical Association,* "Why Do Jesuits Die in Threes?") This trinity is, first of all, free private markets, which includes free trade about which Herbert spoke so eloquently, so that the bulk of economic activity is organized through voluntary cooperation. Fundamentally, it also consists, second, of the free movement of people. Again, the United States, at least when my parents came there, had essentially free movement of people. There were some limitations, but in the main it was free. You cannot have free movement of people in a welfare state. Unfortunately, those two principles conflict. Third, the free movement of money requires either a truly unified currency or truly floating exchange rates. We have neither. Within the continental United States we have unified money, but between countries we have nominally floating exchange rates that are in practice manipulated by governmental central banks, again a subject about which Herbert spoke very well and with which I am in full agreement. We do not need international coordination among central banks. What we need is the abolition of the central banks, not a likely immediate prospect. I say this as no derogation of the people who are in those central banks. Some of them have been my very best friends. Simply listing these requisites shows how far we have yet to go to achieve a truly open society, even in those countries that we tend to lump into the free world.

All three components are both required for and supported by two basic elements. One is limited government and the other is private property. You cannot, in my opinion, have a truly open and free society unless those two basic elements are there. Governments must be limited and property must be private. Those are unduly simple terms. Limited to what? Limited how narrowly? We have discussed that a great deal in our Mont Pèlerin meetings, and many of you in this room have written about that. It clearly is not an easy problem. Yet I believe there is no one who will deny that when government after government—local and central—spends through the treasury 40 to 50 percent of the national income, that's hardly a limited government. When it gets up to 80 percent, as it does in some countries, or over 100 percent, which seems an impossibility but is due to the accounting anomalies involved in computing national income, we surely do not have a limited government.

And private property. Unfortunately, that too is not a simple term; one of the functions of government is to define what private property means. It is very tempting to think that somehow it is a natural right that requires no definition, but it is very far indeed from that.

What about political structure? The word "democracy" is a popular word, and it is a popular word because it means so many different things to so many different people. But the fact is that, if we look over history, a wide variety of political structures have proved consistent with open societies. The open society of which Keynes talked was a constitutional monarchy. His country, Britain, was a constitutional monarchy. The open society that ruled in the United States was a republic. The open society that has been ruling in Hong Kong to a greater extent perhaps than in any other place in the world in the past fifty years has been a colonial enclave. So no manner of political structure has proved incapable of maintaining an open society. That is true both ways. A society can be ostensibly a democracy and yet closed, as has clearly been true in some Latin American countries. A colonial society can be closed. A monarchy can be closed. While we are all acculturated to have particular respect for particular kinds of political structures, the maintenance of an open society depends much more on the beliefs, understanding, and character of the people than it does on the form of institutional structure. The institutional structure does, of course, play a role. I do believe that the existence of the Constitution and the Bill of Rights has played a role in maintaining the United States as a free society. Yet that same Constitution, adopted word for word by some Latin American countries, has not proved capable of maintaining a free and open society. So institutional structure is important, but far more important in my opinion ultimately are the beliefs, understanding, and the character of the people.

In what direction is the world currently headed? There are many hopeful signs, particularly the one I emphasized at the outset, the change in the intellectual climate of opinion that is partly manifested by our having two-hundred-odd people at a Mont Pèlerin meeting in the remote country—relatively remote to most of them—of Japan, something that would have been inconceivable thirty or forty years ago. Nonetheless, it is by no means clear in what direction we are currently headed—whether toward a more open society or toward a more closed society. There is a worldwide movement to privatization, a very good sign, but there is also a worldwide movement to increased protectionism. There is little doubt that protectionism is on the rise and has been for some years now. Herbert emphasized the great leap in world trade and the reduction of barriers during the early postwar decades. But is that going on now? Hardly. If I may take one of his main examples, it is hardly a good sign, as I understand it, that in Germany, which demonstrated the miracle of the market first under Ludwig Erhard, socialist, collectivist, and leftist ideas are again very much on the rise and very important. It is no hopeful sign that in that country, too, government spending is nearly 50 percent of national income.

There is a worldwide move toward lower marginal income tax rates but unfortunately accompanied by what may be even worse systems of taxation. I have in mind two in particular: first, the value-added tax, which economically has much to be said for it but which is politically invisible, and hence inevitably subject to increase and multiplication, so that to the best of my knowledge every country that has a value-added tax has a higher level of government spending relative to income than any country that does not among the advanced countries; second, a form of taxation that is now coming to the fore in the United States, taxation by mandating obligations on private institutions. Senator Kennedy has given up on the hope of national health insurance because President Reagan's unwillingness to raise taxes has produced downward pressure on spending, but he and his fellow resident of Massachusetts, Governor Dukakis, now hope to get national health insurance by mandating that employers provide it. That is a particularly vicious form of taxation because not only is it concealed but it is directed toward a single objective.

There is a great deal of reason for optimism, but there is very little reason for complacency. The task that the Mont Pèlerin Society set for itself, that Friedrich Hayek set for the Mont Pèlerin Society, is very far indeed from having been completed. The task remains and it can demand the best efforts, the best judgment, the best faith of all of us. Thank you.

Note

1. *A Life in Two Centuries* (New York: Stein & Day, 1981), p. 39.

FIFTEEN

THE TIDE IN THE AFFAIRS OF MEN

(1988)

There is a tide in the affairs of men,
Which, taken at the flood, leads on to fortune;
Omitted, all the voyage of their life
Is bound in shallows and in miseries.

—William Shakespeare, *Julius Caesar*

Shakespeare's image is an apt text for our essay. There are powerful tides in the affairs of men, interpreted as the collective entity we call society, just as in the affairs of individuals. The tides in the affairs of society are slow to become apparent, as one tide begins to overrun its predecessor. Each tide lasts a long time—decades, not hours—once it begins to flood and leaves its mark on its successor even after it recedes.

How tides begin in the minds of men, spread to the conduct of public policy, often generate their own reversal, and are succeeded by another tide—all this is a vast topic insufficiently explored by historians, economists, and other social scientists.[1]

The aim of this brief essay is modest: to present a hypothesis that has become increasingly plausible to us over the years, to illustrate it with experience over the past three centuries, and to discuss some of its implications. The hypothesis is that a major change in social and economic policy is preceded by a shift in the climate of intellectual *opinion,* itself generated, at least in part, by contemporaneous social, political, and economic circumstances. This shift may begin in one country but, if it proves lasting, ultimately spreads worldwide. At first it will have little effect on social and economic policy. After a lag, sometimes of decades, an intellectual tide "taken at its flood" will spread at first gradually, then more rapidly, to the public at large and through the public's pressure on government will affect the course of economic, social, and political policy. As the tide in *events* reaches its flood, the intellectual tide starts to ebb, offset by what A. V. Dicey calls countercurrents of opinion. The countercurrents typically represent a reaction to the practical consequences attributed to the earlier intellectual tide. Promise tends to be utopian. Performance never is and therefore disappoints. The initial protagonists of the intellectual tide die out, and the intellectual quality of their followers and supporters inevitably declines. It takes intellectual independence and courage to start a countercurrent to dominant opinion. It takes far less of either to climb on a bandwagon. The venturesome, independent, and courageous young seek new fields to conquer and that calls for exploring the new and untried. The countercurrents that gather force set in motion the next tidal wave, and the process is repeated.

Needless to say, this sketch is oversimplified and excessively formalized. In particular it omits any discussion of the subtle mutual interaction between intellectual opinion, public opinion, and the course of events. Gradual changes in policy and institutional arrangements are always going on. Major changes seldom occur, however, except at times of crisis, when, to use Richard Weaver's evocative phrase, "ideas have consequences." The intellectual tide is spread to the public by all manner of intellectual retailers—teachers and preachers, journalists in print and on television, pundits, and politicians. The public begins to react to the crisis according to the options that intellectuals have explored, options that effectively limit the alternatives open to the powers that be. In almost every tide a crisis can be identified as the catalyst for a major change in the direction of policy.

We shall illustrate the relevance of our hypothesis with the two latest completed tides as well as the tide that, as we put it in the title of the final chapter of *Free to Choose,* is turning.[2]

The Rise of Laissez-Faire
(the Adam Smith Tide)

The first tide we discuss begins in the eighteenth century in Scotland with a reaction against mercantilism expressed in the writings of David Hume, Adam Smith's *Theory of Moral Sentiments* (1759), and above all Smith's *The Wealth of Nations* (1776).

The Wealth of Nations is widely and correctly regarded as the foundation stone of modern scientific economics. Its normative thrust and its influence on the wider intellectual world are of greater interest for our present purpose. Its rapid success in influencing the intellectual community doubtless reflected the seeds planted by Hume and others—the intellectual countercurrents to the mercantilist tide—as well as the early stages of the Industrial Revolution.

On the other side of the Atlantic 1776 also saw the proclamation of the Declaration of Independence—in many ways the political twin of Smith's economics. Smith's work quickly became common currency to the Founding Fathers. Alexander Hamilton documented that phenomenon in a backhanded way in his 1791 *Report on Manufactures.* He quoted Smith extensively and praised him profusely while at the same time devoting the substance of his report to arguing that Smith's doctrines did not apply to the United States, which needed not free international trade but the protection of infant industries by tariffs, an example of the homage that vice, even intellectual vice, pays to virtue.

Smith had no illusions about the impact of his intellectual ideas on public policy: "To expect that the freedom of trade should ever be entirely restored in Great Britain, is as absurd as to expect that an Oceana or Utopia should ever be established in it. Not only the prejudices of the public, but what is much more unconquerable, the private interests of many individuals, irresistibly oppose it."[3]

His prediction proved false. By the early nineteenth century the ideas of laissez-faire, of the operation of the invisible hand, of the undesirability of government intervention into economic matters had swept first the intellectual world and then public policy. Bentham, Ricardo, James Mill, and John Stuart Mill were actively engaged in spreading these ideas and promoting them politically. Maria Edgeworth was writing novels based on Ricardian economics. Cobden and Bright were campaigning for the repeal of the Corn Laws. Reinforced by pressures arising out of the Industrial Revolution, these ideas were beginning to affect public policy, though the process was delayed by the Napoleonic Wars, with the accompanying high government spending and restrictions on international trade. Yet the wars also furnished the needed catalytic crisis.

The repeal of the Corn Laws in 1846 is generally regarded as the final triumph of Smith after a seventy-year delay. In fact some reductions in trade barriers had started much earlier, and many nonagricultural items continued to be protected by tariffs until 1874. Thereafter only revenue tariffs remained on such items as spirits, wine, beer, and tobacco, countervailed by excise duties on competing domestic products. So it took nearly a century for the completion of one response to Adam Smith.

The other countries of Europe and the United States did not follow the British lead by establishing complete free trade in goods. During most of the nineteenth century, however, US duties on imports were primarily for revenue, though protection did play a significant role, as rancorous political debates, particularly between the North and the South, testify. Except for a few years after the War of 1812, customs provided between 90 and 100 percent of total federal revenues up to the Civil War. And except for a few years during and after that war, customs provided half or more of federal revenues until the Spanish-American War at the end of the century.

Nontariff barriers such as quotas were nonexistent. Movement of people and capital was hardly impeded at all. The United States in particular had completely free immigration. In Europe before World War I "the inhabitant of London," in John Maynard Keynes's eloquent words, "could secure . . . cheap and comfortable means of transit to any country or climate without passport or other formality . . . and could . . . proceed abroad to foreign quarters, without knowledge of the religion, language, or customs . . . and would consider himself greatly aggrieved and much surprised at the least interference."[4]

Hamilton's success in achieving protectionist legislation in the United States reflects the absence of effective ideological commitment by policy makers to avoiding intervention by government into economic activity, despite the intellectual tide set in motion by Adam Smith, the French physiocrats, and their later followers. However, strong belief in states' rights meant that states, not the federal government, played the major role. Many states established state banks, built canals, and engaged in other commercial enterprises. The catalytic crisis that produced a drastic change was the panic of 1837, in the course of which many, perhaps most, government enterprises went bankrupt. That panic served the same role in discrediting government enterprise as the Great Depression did nearly a century later in discrediting private enterprise.

In the aftermath the ideas of Adam Smith offered both an explanation and an obvious alternative option; tariffs aside, near complete laissez-faire and nonintervention reigned into the next century.

Measuring the role of government in the economy is not easy. One readily available, though admittedly imperfect, measure is the ratio of government spending to national income. At the height of laissez-faire, peacetime government spending was less than 10 percent of national income in both the United States and Great Britain. Two-thirds of US spending was by state and local governments, with about half for education; federal spending was generally less than 3 percent of national income, with half of that for the military.

A striking example of the worldwide impact of the Adam Smith tide—this time in practice, not in ideas—is provided by post-Meiji Japan. For centuries prior to the Meiji Restoration in 1867, Japan had been almost completely isolated from the Western world. The new rulers had no ideological understanding, let alone commitment, to laissez-faire. On the contrary, they attached little value to individual freedom, either political or economic. Their overriding objective was simply to strengthen the power and glory of their country.

Nevertheless, when the Meiji rulers burst into a Western world in which laissez-faire Britain was the dominant economy, they simply took for granted that Britain's policy was the one to emulate. They did not by any means extend complete economic and political freedom to their citizens, but they did go a long way, with dramatic and highly favorable results.[5]

The absence of a widespread ideological underpinning for these policies helps explain their lack of robustness. After World War I Japan succumbed to centralized control by a military dictatorship—a policy that led to economic stagnation, military adventurism, and finally Japan's entry into World War II on the side of the Nazis.

On a broader scale the tide that swept the nineteenth century brought greater political as well as economic freedom: widening rights and a higher standard of living for individuals accompanied increased international trade and human contact. It was heralded as a century of peace—but that is somewhat overstated. The tide did not prevent the US Civil War, the Crimean War, the Franco-Prussian War, or other local conflicts. But there was no major widespread conflict between 1815 and 1914 comparable either to the Napoleonic Wars of the preceding years or to the world wars of the later years.

Despite occasional financial panics and crises, Britain and the United States experienced remarkable economic growth during the nineteenth century. The United States in particular became a mecca for the poor of all lands. All this was associated with—and many, including us, would say it was a result of—the increasing adoption of laissez-faire as the guiding principle of government policy.

The Rise of the Welfare State
(the Fabian Tide)

This remarkable progress did not prevent the intellectual tide from turning away from individualism and toward collectivism. Indeed, it doubtless contributed to that result. According to Dicey, "from 1848 onwards an alteration becomes perceptible in the intellectual and moral atmosphere of England."[6] The flood stage, when collectivism began to dominate intellectual opinion, came some decades later. The founding of the Fabian Society, dedicated to the gradual establishment of socialism, by George Bernard Shaw, Sidney Webb, and others in 1883, is perhaps as good a dividing date as any for Britain. A comparable date for the United States is 1885, when the American Economic Association was founded by a group of young economists who had returned from study in Germany imbued with socialist ideas, which they hoped to spread through the association—a hope that was largely frustrated when the association shortly adopted a policy of "non-partisanship and avoidance of official commitments on practical economic questions and political issues."[7] Confirming evidence is provided by the publication in 1888 of Edward Bellamy's socialist utopian romance, *Looking Backwards,* which sold over a million copies.

How can we explain this shift in the intellectual tide when the growing pains of laissez-faire policies had long been overcome and impressive positive gains had been achieved? Dicey gives one indirect answer:

> The beneficial effect of State intervention, especially in the form of legislation, is direct, immediate, and, so to speak, visible, whilst its evil effects are gradual and indirect, and lie out of sight . . . few are those who realize the undeniable truth that State help kills self-help. Hence the majority of mankind must almost of necessity look with undue favor upon governmental intervention. This natural bias can be counteracted only by the existence . . . , as in England between 1830 and 1860, of a presumption or prejudice in favor of individual liberty—that is of *laissez-faire*. The mere decline, therefore, of faith in self-help . . . is of itself sufficient to account for the growth of legislation tending toward socialism.[8]

A more direct answer is that two effects of the success of laissez-faire fostered a reaction. First, success made residual evils stand out all the more sharply, both encouraging reformers to press for governmental solutions and making the public more sympathetic to their appeals. Second, it became more reasonable to anticipate that government would be effective in attacking the residual evils. A severely limited government has few favors to give; hence there is little incentive to corrupt government officials, and government service has few attractions for persons concerned primarily with personal enrichment. Government was engaged primarily in enforcing laws against murder, theft, and the like and in providing municipal services such as local police and fire protection—activities that engendered almost unanimous citizen support. For these and other reasons, Britain, which went furthest toward complete laissez-faire, became legendary in the late nineteenth and early twentieth centuries for its incorruptible civil service and law-abiding citizenry—precisely the reverse of its reputation a century earlier. In the United States neither the quality of the civil service nor respect for the law ever reached the heights they did in Britain, but both improved over the course of the century.

Whatever the reasons, Fabian socialism became the dominant intellectual current in Britain, driving out, at the one extreme, radical Marxism, and at the other, laissez-faire. Gradually that intellectual current came to dominate first public opinion and then government policy. World War I hastened the process, but it was already well under way before the war, as is demonstrated by Dicey's prescient remarks in his 1914 preface to the second edition of *Law and Public Opinion:*

> By 1900, the doctrine of *laissez-faire,* in spite of the large element of truth which it contains, had more or less lost its hold upon the English people. . . . It also was in 1900 apparent to any impartial observer that the feelings or the opinions which had given strength to collectivism would continue to tell as strongly upon the legislation of the twentieth century as they already told upon the later legislation of the nineteenth century . . . and this conclusion would naturally have been confirmed by the fact that in the sphere of finance there had occurred a revival of belief in protective tariffs, then known by the name of a demand for "fair trade" [echoes of 1987!].

Dicey lists "the laws which most directly illustrate the progress of collectivism" from the beginning of the twentieth century, starting with the Old Age Pension Act of 1908. In respect of a later act (the Mental Deficiency Act, 1913), he remarks that it "is the first step along a path on which no sane man can decline to enter, but which, if too far pursued, will bring statesmen across difficulties hard to meet without considerable interference with individual liberty."[9]

Clearly the seeds had been sown from which Britain's full-fledged welfare state grew, at first slowly in the interwar period and then with a final burst after World War II, marked perhaps by the adoption of the National Health Service and the panoply of measures recommended in the Beveridge report.

In the United States the development was similar, though somewhat delayed. After the popular success of Bellamy's utopian fantasy came the era of the muckrakers, led by Lincoln Steffens, Ray Stannard Baker, and Ida M. Tarbell, with their exposures of alleged corruption and malfeasance in municipal government, labor, and trusts. Upton Sinclair used the novel to promote socialist ideas, his most successful being *The Jungle* (1906), which resulted from an assignment by a socialist newspaper to investigate conditions in the Chicago stockyards. Sinclair wrote the novel to create sympathy for the workers, but it did far more to arouse indignation at the unsanitary conditions under which meat was processed. On a different level Louis Dembitz Brandeis criticized the financial community. His volume of essays, *Other People's Money and How the Bankers Use It* (1914), has been described as "a frontal assault on monopoly and interlocking directorates."[10]

"The Populist party, through which William Jennings Bryan rose to" the nomination for the presidency on the Democratic ticket in 1896, "called not merely for regulation of the railroads but for outright government ownership and operation."[11] The Interstate Commerce Commission, created in 1887, was shortly followed by the 1890 Sherman Antitrust Act and later by the 1906 Food and Drug Act, for which Sinclair's novel served as the catalyst. The modern welfare state was well on its way. World War I greatly expanded the role of government, notably by the takeover of the railroads. The postwar period brought something of a reaction, with the major exception of Prohibition.

As late as 1929 federal spending amounted to only 3.2 percent of the national income; one-third of this was spent on the military, including veterans' benefits, and one-half on the military plus interest on the public debt. State and local spending was nearly three times as large—9 percent of national income—with more than half on education and highways. Spending by federal, state, and local governments on what today is described as income support, Social Security, and welfare totaled less than 1 percent of national income.

The world of ideas was different. By 1929 socialism was the dominant ideology on the nation's campuses. The *New Republic* and *The Nation* were the intellectual's favorite journals of opinion and Norman Thomas their political hero. The impact of opinion on the world of practice, however, had so far been modest. The critical catalyst for a major change was, of course, the Great Depression, which rightly or wrongly shattered the public's confidence in private enterprise, leading it to regard government involvement as the only effective recourse in time of trouble and to treat government as a potential benefactor rather than simply as a policeman and umpire.

The effect was dramatic. Federal government spending grew to roughly 30 percent of national income by the 1980s, nearly tenfold its 1929 level. State and local spending also grew, though far less dramatically, so that by the 1980s total government spending was over 40 percent of national income. And spending understates the role government came to play. Many intrusions into people's lives involve little or no spending: tariffs and quotas, price and wage controls, ceilings on interest rates, local ceilings on rents, zoning requirements, building codes, and so on.

The delayed impact of the intellectual climate of the 1920s illustrates one aspect of the influence of intellectual opinion—producing options for adoption when the time is ripe. Despite Norman Thomas's popularity on the campus, he received less than 1 percent of the popular vote for president in 1928 and only 2 percent in 1932. Nonetheless, we concluded that "the Socialist party was the most influential political party in the United States in the first decades of the twentieth century. . . . [A]lmost every economic plank in its 1928 presidential platform has by now [1980] been enacted into law."[12]

Like the earlier tide, the Fabian tide was worldwide. It contributed no less to the success of the Russian and Chinese communist revolutions than to the welfare state in Britain and the New Deal in the United States. And it largely explains the adoption of centralized planning in India and other British and European former colonies when they achieved independence. A major exception was Hong Kong, one of the few British colonial possessions that remained under the control of the Colonial Office. It never departed from the Adam Smith tide and as a result was a precursor to the next tide.

The Resurgence of Free Markets (the Hayek Tide)

As in the preceding wave, the world of ideas started to change direction just as the tide in the world of practice was cresting.[13] Throughout the ascendancy of socialist ideas there had, of course, been countercurrents—kept alive in Britain by G. K. Chesterton, Lionel Robbins, Friedrich Hayek, and some of their colleagues at the London School of Economics; in Austria by Ludwig von Mises and his disciples; and in the United States by Albert Jay

Nock, H. L. Mencken, and other popular writers, including Henry Simons, Frank Knight, and Jacob Viner at the University of Chicago and Gottfried Haberler and Joseph Schumpeter at Harvard, to mention only a few.

Hayek's *Road to Serfdom,* a surprise best seller in Britain and in the United States in 1944, was probably the first real inroad in the dominant intellectual view. Yet the impact of the free market countercurrent on the dominant tide of intellectual opinion, though perceptible to those directly involved, was at first minute. Even for those of us who were actively promoting free markets in the 1950s and 1960s it is difficult to recall how strong and pervasive the intellectual climate of the time was.

The tale of two books by the present authors, both directed at the general public and both promoting the same policies, provides striking evidence of the change in the climate of opinion. The first, *Capitalism and Freedom,* published in 1962 and destined to sell more than 400,000 copies in the next eighteen years, was not reviewed at the time in a single popular American periodical: not in the *New York Times,* the *Chicago Tribune, Newsweek, Time,* you name it. The second, *Free to Choose,* published in 1980, was reviewed by every major publication (by some more than once), became the year's best-selling nonfiction book in the United States, and received worldwide attention.

Further evidence of the change in the intellectual climate is the proliferation of think tanks promoting the ideas of limited government and reliance on free markets. In a recent talk Ed Feulner, president of the Heritage Foundation, could mention only four that existed three decades ago: the Hoover Institution, still here today; the Intercollegiate Society of Individualists, which has changed its name but kept the initials; an embryonic American Enterprise Institute; and the Center for Strategic and International Studies. He should also have included Leonard Read's Foundation for Economic Education (FEE).

By contrast, Feulner noted a long list of additional institutions currently devoted to developing and spreading the idea of limited government and free markets, plus a host of others trying to translate ideas into action. The same contrast is true of publications. FEE's *Freeman* was the only one he or we can think of that was promoting the ideas of freedom thirty to forty years ago. Today numerous publications promote these ideas, though with great differences in specific areas: *Freeman, National Review, Human Events, American Spectator, Policy Review,* and *Reason.* Even the *New Republic* and the *Nation* are no longer the undeviating proponents of socialist orthodoxy that they were three decades ago.

Why this great shift in public attitudes? The persuasive power of such books as Friedrich Hayek's *Road to Serfdom,* Ayn Rand's *Fountainhead, Atlas Shrugged,* our own *Capitalism and Freedom,* and numerous others led people to think about the problem in a different way and to become aware that government failure was as real as market failure. Nevertheless, we conjecture that the extraordinary force of experience was the major reason for the change.

Experience turned the great hopes that the collectivists and socialists had placed in Russia and China to ashes. Indeed, the only hope in those countries comes from recent moves toward the free market. Similarly experience dampened, to put it mildly, the extravagant hopes placed in Fabian socialism and the welfare state in Britain and in the New Deal in the United States. One major government program after another, each started with the best of intentions, resulted in more problems than solutions.

Few today still regard nationalization of enterprises as a way to promote more efficient production. Few still believe that every social problem can be solved by throwing government (that is, taxpayer) money at it. In these areas liberal ideas—in the original nineteenth-century meaning of liberal—have won the battle. The neoconservatives are correct in defining themselves as (modern) liberals mugged by reality. They still retain many of their earlier values but have been driven to recognize that they cannot achieve them through government.

In this country the Vietnam War helped to undermine belief in the beneficence of government. And most of all, as Dicey predicted nearly seventy-five years ago, the rising burden of taxation caused the general public to react against the growth of government and its spreading influence.[14]

In both the United States and Britain respect for the law declined in the twentieth century under the impact of the widening scope of government, strongly reinforced in the United States by Prohibition. The growing range of favors governments could give led to a steady increase in what economists have come to call rent seeking and what the public refers to as special-interest lobbying.

Worldwide the contrast between the stagnation of those poorer countries that engaged in central planning (India, the former African colonies, Central American countries) and the rapid progress of the few that followed a largely free market policy (notably the Four Tigers of the Far East: Hong Kong, Singapore, Taiwan, and South Korea) strongly reinforced the experience of the advanced countries of the West.

Ideas played a significant part, as in earlier episodes, less by persuading the public than by keeping options open, providing alternative policies to adopt when changes had to be made.

As in the two earlier waves, practice has lagged far behind ideas, so that both Britain and the United States are further from the ideal of a free society than they were thirty to forty years ago in almost every dimension. In 1950 spending by US federal, state, and local governments was 25 percent of national income; in 1985 it was 44 percent. In the past thirty years a host of new government agencies has been created: a Department of Education, a National Endowment for the Arts and another for the humanities, Environmental Protection Agency, Occupational Safety and

Health Administration, and so on. Civil servants in these and many additional agencies decide for us what is in our best interest.

Nonetheless, practice has started to change. The catalytic crisis sparking the change was, we believe, the worldwide wave of inflation during the 1970s, originating in excessively expansive monetary growth in the United States in the 1960s. That episode was catalytic in two respects: first, stagflation destroyed the credibility of Keynesian monetary and fiscal policy and hence of the government's capacity to fine-tune the economy; second, it brought into play Dicey's "weight of taxation" through bracket creep and the implicit repudiation of government debt.

Already in the 1970s military conscription was terminated, airlines deregulated, and regulation Q, which limited the interest rates that banks could pay on deposits, eliminated. In 1982 the Civil Aeronautics Board that regulated the airlines was eliminated. Though government spending as a fraction of national income has continued to rise, the rate of increase has slowed. No major new spending programs have been passed since 1981. The increase in nonmilitary government spending has been predominantly the effect of earlier programs.

As in earlier waves, the tides of both opinion and practice have swept worldwide. Britain went further in the direction of collectivism than the United States and still remains more collectivist—with both a higher ratio of government spending to national income and far more extensive nationalization of industry. Yet Britain has made more progress under Margaret Thatcher than the United States has under Ronald Reagan.

Equally impressive are changes in the communist world. Even there it was impossible to repress all countercurrents, as Solzhenitsyn, Sakharov, and many other brave men and women so eloquently testify. But beyond the countercurrents, the economic reforms in Hungary, Solidarity in Poland, the widened resort to markets in China, the current reformist talk in the Soviet

Union—these owe as much to the force of events and the options kept open by intellectual ideas as do the election of Margaret Thatcher and Ronald Reagan in the West. True, it is doubtful that such reforms will be permitted to go far enough to threaten the power of the current political elite. But that does not lessen their value as testimony to the power of ideas.

One interesting and instructive phenomenon is that freeing the market has been equally or more vigorously pursued under ostensibly left-wing governments as under ostensibly right-wing governments. Communist countries aside, one striking example is the U-turn in French policy brought about by Mitterrand, a life-long socialist. In Australia a Labour government replaced a conservative government and then moved sharply to widen the role of the market. New Zealand, under a Labour government headed by David Lange, first elected in 1984 and reelected in 1987, has gone further than any other country in dismantling government controls and economic intervention.

By contrast, Germany, though it owed its dramatic post–World War II recovery to the free market policies of Ludwig Erhard, has steadily moved away from those policies, first under a Social Democratic government and, more recently, under conservative governments. Can the explanation for this aberration be that the dramatic move to free market policies was primarily the result of one man's (Erhard's) actions and not of a change in public opinion?

All in all the force of ideas, propelled by the pressure of events, is clearly no respecter of geography or ideology or party label.

Conclusion

We have surveyed briefly two completed pairs of tides in the climate of opinion and the "affairs of men" and one pair still in progress. Each tide lasted between fifty and a hundred years. First came the tide in the climate of public opinion: toward free markets and laissez-faire from, say, 1776 to 1883 in Britain, 1776 to 1885 in the United States; toward collectivism from 1883 to 1950 in Britain, from 1885 to 1970 in the United States. Some decades later came the tide in the "affairs of men": toward laissez-faire from, say, 1820 to 1900 in Britain, 1840 to 1930 in the United States; toward collectivism from, say, 1900 to 1978 in Britain, 1930 to 1980 in the United States. Needless to say, these are only the roughest of dates. They could easily be set a decade or so earlier or later.

Two new pairs of tides are now in their rising phases: in public opinion, toward renewed reliance on markets and more limited government, beginning in about 1950 in Britain and 1970 in the United States; in public policy, beginning in 1978 in Britain and 1980 in the United States and even more recently in other countries.

If the completed tides are any guide, the current wave in opinion is approaching middle age and in public policy is still in its infancy. Both are therefore still rising and the flood stage, certainly in affairs, is yet to come.

For those who believe in a free society and a narrowly limited role for government, that is reason for optimism. But it is not a reason for complacency. Nothing is inevitable about the course of history—however it may appear in retrospect. "Because we live in a largely free society, we tend to forget how limited is the span of time and the part of the globe for which there has ever been anything like political freedom: the typical state of mankind is tyranny, servitude, and misery."[15]

The encouraging tide in affairs that is in its infancy can still be aborted, can be overwhelmed by a renewed tide of collectivism. The expanded role of government even in Western societies that pride themselves in being part of the free world has created many vested interests that will strongly resist the loss of privileges that they have come to regard as their right. Everyone is capable of believing that what is good for oneself is good for the country and therefore of justifying a special exception to a general rule that we all profess to favor.

Yet the lesson of the two earlier waves is clear: once a tide in opinion or in affairs is strongly set, it tends to overwhelm countercurrents and to keep going for a long time in the same direction. The tides are capable of ignoring geography, political labels, and other hindrances to their continuance. Yet it is also worth recalling that their very success tends to create conditions that may ultimately reverse them.

Notes

1. A British constitutional-law scholar has written the most insightful book on the subject: A. V. Dicey, *Lectures on the Relation between Law and Public Opinion in England during the Nineteenth Century,* 2d ed. (London: Macmillan, 1914).

2. Milton Friedman and Rose D. Friedman, *Free to Choose* (New York and London: Harcourt Brace Jovanovich, 1980), p. 283.

3. Adam Smith, *The Wealth of Nations,* Cannan, 5th ed. (London: Methuen, 1930), bk. 4, chap. 2, p. 43.

4. J. M. Keynes, *Economic Consequences of the Peace* (London: Macmillan, 1919), pp. 6, 7, 9.

5. See Friedman and Friedman, *Free to Choose,* pp. 59, 61–62.

6. Dicey, *Law and Public Opinion,* p. 245.

7. A. W. Coats, "The American Economics Association and the Economics Profession," *Journal of Economic Literature* 23 (December 1985): 1702.

8. Dicey, *Law and Public Opinion,* pp. 257–58.

9. Ibid., pp. xxxi, xxxii, xxxiii, li.

10. *Encyclopaedia Britannica,* 1970 ed., s.v. "Brandeis, Louis Dembitz."

11. Friedman and Friedman, *Free to Choose,* p. 196.

12. Ibid., pp. 286, 287.

13. This section is based partly on Milton Friedman, "Where Are We on the Road to Liberty?" *Reason* 19, no. 2 (June 1987): 31–33.

14. "[I]f the progress of socialistic legislation be arrested, the check will be due, not so much to the influence of any thinker as to some patent fact which shall command public attention; such, for instance, as that increase in the weight of taxation which is apparently the usual, if not the invariable, concomitant of a socialistic policy" (Dicey, *Law and Public Opinion,* p. 302n).

15. Milton Friedman, with the assistance of Rose D. Friedman, *Capitalism and Freedom* (Chicago: University of Chicago Press, 1962), p. 9.

BIBLIOGRAPHICAL NOTES

1. LIBERALISM, OLD STYLE

In *1955 Collier's Year Book,* pp. 360–63. New York: P. F. Collier
& Son, 1955. Reprinted in *The Indispensable Milton Friedman:
Essays on Politics and Economics,* edited by Lanny Ebenstein,
pp. 11–24. Washington, DC: Regnery Publishing, 2012. Copyright
© 1955 by Milton Friedman. Reprinted courtesy of the Friedman
family.

2. THE RELATION BETWEEN ECONOMIC FREEDOM AND POLITICAL FREEDOM

In *Capitalism and Freedom,* by Milton Friedman, chapter 1,
pp. 7–21. Chicago: University of Chicago Press, 1962. Earlier ver-
sions published as (1) "Capitalism and Freedom," in *Essays on
Individuality,* edited by Felix Morley, pp. 168–82. Philadelphia:
University of Pennsylvania, 1958. (2) "Capitalism and Freedom,"
New Individualist Review 1 (April 1961): 3–10. Condensation
reprinted as "Capitalism and Freedom: Why and How the Two Ideas
Are Mutually Dependent," *Wall Street Journal,* 17 May 1961, and
"The New Liberal's Creed: Individual Freedom, Preserving Dissent
Are Ultimate Goods," *Wall Street Journal,* 18 May 1961. Excerpts
reprinted with discussion in *Freedom, Democracy, and Economic
Welfare: Proceedings of an International Symposium,* edited by
Michael A. Walker, pp. 51–56. Vancouver, British Columbia: Fraser
Institute, 1988. Copyright © 1962, 1982, 2002 by the University of
Chicago. All rights reserved. Reprinted with permission.

3. THE ROLE OF GOVERNMENT IN A FREE SOCIETY

In *Capitalism and Freedom,* by Milton Friedman, chapter 2, pp. 22–36.
Chicago: University of Chicago Press, 1962. Condensation reprinted in
*Friedman and Szasz on Liberty and Drugs: Essays on the Free Market
and Prohibition,* edited by Arnold S. Trebach and Kevin B. Zeese,
pp. 7–13. Washington, DC: Drug Policy Foundation Press, 1992. Based
on the lecture "The Role of Government in a Liberal Society," Wabash
College, June 1956. Copyright © 1962, 1982, 2002 by the University of
Chicago. All rights reserved. Reprinted with permission.

4. IS A FREE SOCIETY STABLE?

New Individualist Review 2 (Summer 1962): 3–10. Copyright © 1962 by
Liberty Fund, Inc. Reprinted courtesy of the *New Individualist Review*
and Liberty Fund, Inc.

5. AN INTERVIEW WITH MILTON FRIEDMAN

Interviewed by Tibor Machan, Joe Cobb, and Ralph Raico. *Reason,*
December 1974, pp. 4–14. Copyright © 1974 by the Reason Foundation.
All rights reserved.

6. SAY "NO" TO INTOLERANCE

Liberty 4 (July 1991): 17–18, 20. Edited transcript of an address at
the Future of Freedom Conference of the International Society for
Individual Liberty, San Francisco, 14 August 1990. Copyright © 1991
Liberty Foundation. Appears courtesy of *Liberty* magazine.

7. THE LINE WE DARE NOT CROSS

Encounter, November 1976, pp. 8–14. Excerpts reprinted as (1) "What
Friedman Really Thinks of Britain," *The Sunday Telegraph,* 31 October
1976. (2) "The Path We Dare Not Take," *Reader's Digest,* March 1977,
pp. 110–15. (3) "The Threat to Freedom in the Welfare State," *Business
and Society Review,* no. 21 (Spring 1977), pp. 8–16. Revised versions

published as (1) "The Fragility of Freedom," *Brigham Young University Studies* 16 (Summer 1976): 561–74. (2) "The Fragility of Freedom," *Milton Friedman in South Africa,* edited by Meyer Feldberg, Kate Jowell, and Stephen Mulholland, pp. 3–10. Cape Town: University of Cape Town Graduate School of Business; and Johannesburg: *The Sunday Times,* 1976. Reprinted courtesy of the Friedman family.

8. THE FUTURE OF CAPITALISM

Malibu, California: Pepperdine University Associates, 1977. Reprinted in (1) *Vital Speeches* 43 (March 15, 1977): 333–37. (2) *Reason,* May 1978, pp. 18–21, 61. (3) *Tax Limitation, Inflation and the Role of Government,* by Milton Friedman, pp. 1–13. Dallas, Texas: The Fisher Institute, 1978. Address at Pepperdine University, 9 February 1977. Reprinted courtesy of the Pepperdine University Speeches Collection, Pepperdine University Special Collections and University Archives.

9. FAIR VERSUS FREE

Newsweek, July 4, 1977, p. 70. Reprinted in (1) *Bright Promises, Dismal Performance,* by Milton Friedman, pp. 91–93, edited by William R. Allen. New York: Harcourt Brace Jovanovich, 1983. (2) *The Essence of Friedman,* edited by Kurt R. Leube, pp. 146–47. Stanford, California: Hoover Institution Press, 1987. Originally delivered as a commencement address at Virginia Polytechnic Institute, 28 May 1977. Copyright © 1977 Newsweek/Daily Beast Company LLC. All rights reserved.

10. CREATED EQUAL

In *Free to Choose, A Personal Statement,* by Milton Friedman and Rose D. Friedman, chapter 5, pp. 128–49. New York: Harcourt Brace Jovanovich, 1980. Copyright © 1980 by Milton Friedman and Rose D. Friedman. Reprinted courtesy of the Friedman family.

11. THE MEANING OF FREEDOM

West Point, New York: United States Military Academy, 1985. Edited
version of the twelfth Sol Feinstone Lecture on "The Meaning
of Freedom," presented at the United States Military Academy,
26 September 1984. Reprinted courtesy of the Friedman family.

12. FREE MARKETS AND FREE SPEECH

Originally published in *Harvard Journal of Law & Public Policy* 10
(Winter 1987): 1–9. Reprinted with permission.

13. WHERE ARE WE ON THE ROAD TO LIBERTY?

Reason, June 1987, pp. 31–33. Adaptation of an address at the Reason
Foundation's Welcome-to-Los Angeles banquet, 18 October 1986.
Copyright © 1987 by the Reason Foundation. All rights reserved.

14. THE FOUNDATIONS OF A FREE SOCIETY

Keynote Address and Nobel Prize Memorial Lecture, General Meeting
of the Mont Pèlerin Society, Toyko, Japan, 5 September 1988. Reprinted
courtesy of the Mont Pèlerin Society/Foundation for Economic
Education.

15. THE TIDE IN THE AFFAIRS OF MEN

Written with Rose D. Friedman, in *Thinking about America: The
United States in the 1990s,* edited by Annelise Anderson and Dennis
L. Bark, pp. 455–68. Stanford, California: Hoover Institution Press,
1988. Copyright © 1988 by the Board of Trustees of the Leland
Stanford Junior University. Reprinted in (1) *The Freeman,* April 1989,
pp. 135–43. (2) *The Indispensable Milton Friedman: Essays on Politics
and Economics,* edited by Lanny Ebenstein, pp. 59–76. Washington,
DC: Regnery Publishing, 2012.

ABOUT MILTON FRIEDMAN

The recipient of the 1976 Nobel Memorial Prize in Economic Sciences, Milton Friedman was a senior research fellow at the Hoover Institution from 1977 to 2006. He was also the Paul Snowden Russell Distinguished Service Professor Emeritus of Economics at the University of Chicago, where he taught from 1946 to 1976, and a member of the research staff of the National Bureau of Economic Research from 1937 to 1981. Milton Friedman was a member of the American Philosophical Society, the National Academy of Sciences, and the Econometric Society.

Friedman was widely regarded as the leader of the Chicago School of monetary economics, which stresses the importance of the quantity of money as an instrument of government policy and as a determinant of business cycles and inflation. He published many books and articles, most notably *A Theory of the Consumption Function, The Optimum Quantity of Money and Other Essays,* and (with A. J. Schwartz) *A Monetary History of the United States, Monetary Statistics of the United States,* and *Monetary Trends in the United States and the United Kingdom.*

In addition to his scientific work, Friedman wrote extensively on public policy, always with the primary emphasis on the preservation and extension of individual freedom. His most important books in this field are *Capitalism and Freedom* (1962), with the assistance of his wife, Rose D. Friedman; *Bright Promises, Dismal Performance* (1983), which consists mostly of reprints of columns he wrote for *Newsweek* from 1966 to 1983; *Free to Choose* (1980), co-authored with his wife Rose D. Friedman, which complemented a ten-part television series of the same name shown on the Public Broadcasting Service (PBS) network in early 1980; and, with Rose D. Friedman, *Tyranny of the Status Quo* (1984), which complemented a three-part television series of the same name shown on PBS in early 1984. *Two Lucky People: Memoirs,* also coauthored with his wife, was published in 1998.

Milton Friedman was awarded the Presidential Medal of Freedom in 1988 and received the National Medal of Science the same year.

ABOUT THE EDITORS

Robert Leeson

Robert Leeson is a prolific historian of economic thought who has published or edited more than twenty books on Milton Friedman, A. W. H. Phillips, and Friedrich Hayek. He has served as a visiting professor of economics at Stanford University and at the University of Trento, adjunct professor of economics at the University of Notre Dame Australia, and visiting fellow at the Hoover Institution, Stanford University. He was previously Bradley Fellow at the University of Western Ontario, and was a W. Glenn Campbell and Rita Ricardo-Campbell National Fellow for 2006–2007 at the Hoover Institution. For the last quarter of a century he has been investigating the dynamics of macroeconomic policy formation. He has published in numerous top-class journals, including the *Economic Journal, Economica, The Cambridge Journal of Economics,* and the *History of Political Economy.*

Charles G. Palm

Charles G. Palm is the deputy director emeritus of the Hoover Institution at Stanford University. Retiring in 2002, he completed thirty-one years of service at Hoover, including eighteen years directing the Hoover Library & Archives. His positions at Hoover included deputy director, 1990–2002; associate director, 1987–90; head librarian, 1986–87; archivist, 1984–87; deputy archivist, 1974–84; and assistant archivist, 1971–74.

In 1992 Palm negotiated an agreement between Hoover and the Russian State Archival Service to microfilm the archives of the Soviet Communist Party and Soviet State, totaling more than twelve million documents dating from the founding of the party in 1898 to the collapse of the Soviet Union in 1991. He also led a collecting effort to acquire records on communism and the transition to democracy in Eastern Europe after the fall of the Berlin Wall in 1989, resulting in the acquisition of 2.5 tons of materials for Hoover. Among other collections acquired by Palm are the papers of Friedrich Hayek, Milton Friedman, and Karl Popper, as well as the archives of Radio Free Europe/Radio Liberty, William F. Buckley's *Firing Line,* and the Mont Pelerin Society.

He was appointed by President George H. W. Bush to the National Historical Publications and Records Commission in 1990 and served until 1996 and by Governor George Deukmejian to the California Heritage Preservation Commission in 1988, for which he served as chairman from 1997 to 2004. He also served on the History and Education Center Advisory Board of the American Red Cross and the Golden State Museum Corporation. Palm is a fellow of the Society of American Archivists and past president of the Society of California Archivists.

ABOUT JOHN B. TAYLOR

John B. Taylor is the Mary and Robert Raymond Professor of Economics at Stanford University, the George P. Shultz Senior Fellow in Economics at Stanford's Hoover Institution, and the director of Stanford's Introductory Economics Center. He served as senior economist on the president's Council of Economic Advisers and as a member of the council. From 2001 to 2005, he served as undersecretary of the Treasury for international affairs. Taylor was awarded the university-wide Hoagland Prize and the Rhodes Prize for excellence in undergraduate teaching and the Stanford Economics Department's Distinguished Faculty Teaching Award. He received the 2016 Adam Smith Award from the Association of Private Enterprise Education, the Truman Medal for Economic Policy for extraordinary contribution to the formation and conduct of economic policy, the Bradley Prize for his economic research and policy achievements, the Adam Smith Award from the National Association for Business Economics, the Alexander Hamilton Award and the Treasury Distinguished Service Award for his policy contributions at the US Treasury, and the Medal of the Republic of Uruguay for his work in resolving the 2002 financial crisis. Taylor received a BA in economics summa cum laude from Princeton University and a PhD in economics from Stanford. He won the 2012 Hayek Prize for his book *First Principles: Five Keys to Restoring America's Prosperity*.

INDEX